COVERS & JACKETS!

LIBRARY OF APPLIED DESIGN

An Imprint of
PBC International, Inc.

STEVEN HELLER & ANNE FINK

COVERS & JACKETS!

WHAT THE BEST DRESSED BOOKS & MAGAZINES ARE WEARING

Distributor to the book trade in the United States and Canada

Rizzoli International Publications Inc.

300 Park Avenue South

New York, NY 10010

Distributor to the art trade in the United States and Canada

PBC International, Inc.

One School Street

Glen Cove, NY 11542

1-800-527-2826

Fax 516-676-2738

Distributor throughout the rest of the world

Hearst Books International

1350 Avenue of the Americas

New York, NY 10019

Library Of Congress Cataloging–in–Publication Data

Heller, Steven

        Covers & Jackets! : what the best dressed books and magazines are wearing

/ by Steven Heller & Anne Fink.

        p.   cm.

Includes index.

ISBN 0-86636-195-2

1. Book jackets--Catalogs. 2. Magazine covers--United States-- Catalogs.

I. Fink, Anne. II. Title. III. Title: covers and jackets.

NC973.5.U6M45   1993   92-38296

741.6'4'09048--dc20   CIP

                                (Pbk ISBN 0-86636-286-x)

CAVEAT– Information in this text is believed accurate, and will pose

no problem for the student or casual reader. However, the author was

often constrained by information contained in signed release forms,

information that could have been in error or not included at all. Any

misinformation (or lack of information) is the result of failure

in these attestations. The author has done whatever is possible to insure

accuracy.

Design by Stephanie Tevonian

Printed in China

10 9 8 7 6 5 4 3 2 1

To Nick

CONTENTS

DESIGNING THROUGH THE GAUNTLET

Book jackets, paperback covers, and magazine covers
have only one thing in common: They sell. No other component of book or magazine design is so
directly targeted at the consumer, and therefore as scrutinized by marketing, advertising, and distribution experts. Even seasoned veterans find designing a book jacket, paperback cover, or magazine cover can be like running a gauntlet with editors on the one side and marketing people on
the other. Owing to such hazards it should come as no surprise that the majority of what greets
the public in bookstores and on newsstands today may in fact be eye-catching, but has the creativity beaten out of it. Every designer who has been through the mill knows that committees are bad
clients. Despite the constraints on creativity, however, some exemplary book jacket, paperback
cover, and magazine cover design has been produced during the past five years. This book is a celebration of the most accomplished design from this period selected from a variety of countries.

While the problems in designing book jackets, paperback covers, and magazine covers are
sometimes similar, the two forms are, for the most part, worlds apart. Because they share only
one real defining feature—as points of sale—each discipline must be judged by different marketing, if not design standards; hence, one must examine the inherent contrasts between the two
forms and the contexts in which they are found. The bookstore and newsstand (even when under
the same roof) are totally different theaters of retail operation. While both display large invento-
ries—where each product vies for public attention—the marketing of a periodical requires a
decidedly different mindset than a book. Although both are often savagely competitive fields,
books and magazines satisfy very different intellectual, educational, and even emotional needs.
A magazine is ephemeral, a book (even if it is only read once) is not.

This does not mean that magazines are purchased only on impulse and books only after extended deliberation. Habit dictates many magazine sales, and emotion governs many book sales. The particulars involved in designing book and magazine fronts are often based on perceived (or systematically determined) consumer browsing and buying patterns observed over long periods. Sometimes these contribute to intractable, often stultifying rules. But saving the critiques for later, let us look at how these media are sold to the public and why the rules are made. Traditionally a newsstand magazine is targeted first at loyal readers on the basis of its sustained reputation, and second at the casual reader on the strength of the content of a specific issue. New magazines must trade off their novelty to gain initial attention, but must ultimately build upon strong contents to maintain and transcend that first surge of interest. Although many magazines' circulation relies on subscriptions, newsstand sales are a key factor in determining advertising rates, and moreover, contribute to how many subscriptions a magazine might ultimately garner. Therefore magazine covers must be like flowers to the bee, and attract attention in any manner. Books, on the other hand, require completely different sales strategies based first on the obvious fact that they are not periodicals, and second on how the market is apportioned; for example, distinct buying patterns apply for hardcover fiction as opposed to paperback fiction, or popular nonfiction as opposed to serious nonfiction. Depending on the subject, a book may either be an impulse or a more deliberate purchase. In either case a book—whether hardcover or paperback—is more often than not sold on the reputation of the author and/or the allure of the subject. Furthermore, book sales are aided by critical reviews (some marketing experts argue that even a bad review is good publicity) which often influence the consumer more than any other inducement, including the jacket or cover. A magazine rarely generates the same kind of "free" public relations, and therefore must rely on paid outside or self-contained advertising often in the form of coverlines.

The way books and magazines are distributed to retail stores is also a consideration in determining the look of the product. A magazine is often distributed together with a large inventory of other periodicals. The news dealer usually accepts what the distributor offers, depending on the capacity of the newsstand to absorb the quantity of titles. Although a good cover is not shunned, cover design is not a significant factor in whether a news dealer will take a magazine; rather this decision is based on whether the retailer can sell an allotted number of copies. Conversely, books are sold to bookstores by sales representatives ostensibly on a book by book basis—shelf space is too limited and valuable for a retailer to take everything. So here alluring jackets and covers are important selling points for the retailer, especially when an author is unknown or a subject is arcane. Of course what is alluring is a matter of taste or whim, yet with sales in the balance sales representatives have been known to exert extreme pressure on the jacket or cover design of a book.

A magazine often competes with other magazines in the same genre. Since news, fashion, style, and culture magazines are crowded fields, and buyers rarely sample them all, competition can be fierce. Therefore magazines are usually laden with coverline inducements. Coverlines are the bane of the designer when it means junking-up good photographs or illustrations as is often the case. Conversely, a book usually does not have to compete within its genre (with notable exceptions of books in the competitive cooking, gardening, how-to, and travel markets), but must nevertheless command attention on crowded shelves. With books there is general agreement that a jacket or cover should serve as a mini-poster, therefore books are generally not as typographically burdened as magazine covers; moreover, jacket flaps and back cover advertising text do the same job.

Differences do exist, however, between how hardcovers and paperbacks are sold. Within these specific genres differences in design approaches are imposed between the sub-genres like trade and mass market paperbacks, literature and pop fiction, nonfiction and infotainment, etc. Every genre seems to be saddled with its own traditions, taboos, and superstitions which are upheld by marketing experts throughout the world. Sometimes they make sense, other times not. Even when they make sense—for example, the so-called "ten foot rule" that the title of a book should be read from that distance, or that for pop fiction the author's name must take up one-third the image area—they can still have deleterious effects on the way that covers are designed. Magazines suffer from similar, arbitrary decrees—including such ideas as the color blue should never be used in a logo, or that white backgrounds are forbidden. In both disciplines conforming to capricious dictates often results in cliché solutions.

Yet, in spite of the routine problems, excellent work is produced when talent, imagination, skill, and trust, are exercised on both editorial and marketing sides. Trust is the key. If all the other factors are there, then with trust the art director, designer, editor, publisher, and marketer should work in harmony to produce exemplary work.

The above cautionary notes and critiques to the contrary, this book is a celebration of successful design, often the result of exceptional vision. But it must also be stated that the qualitative standard by which a jacket or cover is included here is not based on how well a book or magazine has sold, but rather was an aesthetically pleasing and/or intelligently challenging book jacket and cover and magazine cover produced. In this sense the work here is judged at face value. The book is divided into two major parts—books and magazines—with examples organized according to their sub-genres. However, even though the tendency is to compare, it is not the author's intent to analyze why one works better than the next. Think of this as a sampler of achievement; and that a piece has been included indicates that its designer has successfully run the gauntlet.

  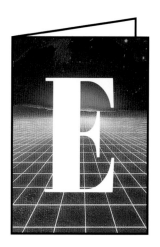 

It's tempting to begin this discussion of book jackets and covers with a familiar old saying, but since everyone would agree that the content of a book cannot be totally defined or even summarized by its jacket or cover it's unnecessary. Despite some marketing experts' attempts to squeeze as much information onto a cover or jacket as could possibly fit, the most that can be adequately conveyed is the title, author, and where an image is used, an abstract of the subject. At their most utilitarian, jackets and covers sell a product; at their most artistic, they establish an aura through type and image. The worst covers and jackets are laden with too many graphic elements; the best are imbued with the same aesthetic virtues as the most masterful advertising posters—and indeed are mini-posters. For decades the publishing industry has supported and produced both kinds; the former is often the result of extensive interference by publishers who invoke hard-sell marketing formulas, while the latter usually springs from designers with taste and vision who reject such constraints.

Despite the thousands of formulaic book jackets and covers published annually, this design genre is actually a wellspring of exciting, often innovative activity. A decade ago, before the advent of the CD, record album designers blazed trails with experimental graphics and pyrotechnic designs. Today book jackets, and more than ever, paperback covers, are on the one hand pushing the boundaries of image-making, while on the other proving that exquisite neoclassical design is still viable. The hippie record buyers of the seventies are the yuppie book buyers of the nineties, and not surprisingly many young book jacket and cover designers are creating packages that have evolved directly from record album aesthetics. Like record packaging, many books today, especially in the fiction category, are marketed to audiences who have come to expect that art and design will complement rather than mimic the content. Communication through abstraction is the rule. And the most exceptional new designs are imbued with visual codes and styles that purposely, and often aggressively signal contemporaneity.

This was not always true. The book jacket, which was introduced in London, England, in 1833 by Longmans & Co., took decades to evolve from a protective cover to an advertisement, and ultimately into an art form. The first jackets were intended to keep the corrosive effects of dust and light at bay. Heavy paper was wrapped around and folded into the cloth binding (the true cover of a book) and was usually discarded after purchase. For about 50 years afterward the covering, known as the dust jacket, was exclusively utilitarian—a plain wrapper with a small window cut out to reveal the title and author's name. It was the standard until the 1890s when, according to historian Steven Greengard, "...decorative consideration was accorded the trade binding with more regularity." A variety of well-known graphic artists were commissioned to render decorative motifs that were stamped or embossed on the cover itself. Soon publishers had these same designs printed on the paper jacket for advertising and eye appeal. By the turn of the century the dust jacket was the publishing industry's primary promotion tool, but was nevertheless still considered a disposable wrapper.

Orthodox book designers often refused to do jackets asserting that it was merely a marketing appendage and not an integral part of the book and binding design. During the early twentieth century the design of a book jacket was often the task of the journeyman layout artist or advertising illustrator (many of whom did not even sign their work). As the production of books for a mass market grew during the teens and twenties, however, the art and design of jackets gradually improved. Many of the same fashionable graphic conceits and mannerisms that were used to sell commodities were applied to book jacket design, often resulting in better display and increased sales. Eventually, jacket artists began taking credit for their work as certain publishers in the United States and Europe took the medium more seriously as an art form.

Although book jackets, and later paperback covers, became a moderately profitable outlet for illustrators and designers during the 1930s, this should by no means be considered the golden age of the form, but rather a period of adolescence which at its best was driven by attractive styles, and at worst was laden with the same excesses that afflicted other forms of advertising. With the notable exceptions of jackets designed by American moderns Alvin Lustig and Paul Rand in the late 1940s most jacket design worldwide took an aesthetic nosedive from the forties through the mid-1950s, owing to changes in graphic style as well as marketing practices. Conversely, the paperback, which premiered during the late twenties and grew in popularity as an inexpensive and portable alternative to expensive and cumbersome hardcovers (especially in the United States) during the forties, was so deliberately hard-sell that its art and design developed into an art form that was known for distinctive romance and adventure paintings on some and commercial surrealism on other fiction and nonfiction titles.

During the fifties book covers as a rule either adopted the dominant styles of sentimental illustration used for magazines and advertising or were bold, no-nonsense type treatments. There were exceptions. The young moderns who adhered to Bauhaus and Swiss principles of correct form practiced a rational simplicity that provided a jarringly elegant alternative to the hard-sell state of the art. By the sixties book jackets and covers began to reject the aesthetic and philosophical diversity of graphic design in general, simply defined as a difference between modern and eclectic approaches. This distinction can be illustrated in American publishing by comparing an exponent of the Swiss school like Rudolph DeHarak, who created masterpieces of economy using only one typeface against a stark symbolic image, often printed in only two colors, with Milton Glaser, whose Push Pin Studios was a proponent of the eclectic approach, and who comixed idiosyncratic illustration and typography into a distinctive period style (which had impact in the United States and Europe). Also emerging during this time was a convention known as the "bestseller style," invented by Paul Bacon whose fundamental approach involved a large headline (title and author) complemented by a small, but beautifully rendered painting that showed a symbolic scene. Bacon's work for various pubishers, which was borrowed or copied by many others, established the standard for a certain genre of popular, contemporary books that continues to this day.

Graphic styles change as rapidly in the world of publishing as in any commercial enterprise that requires regeneration to stay fresh and current. Sometimes this occurs by accident, other times by design. Back-listed books are routinely given new covers and jackets to goose a new generation of consumers into buying the ancient and modern classics. But for at least a generation during the sixties and seventies much of the book jacket and cover design in the United States and Europe was governed by strict marketing conventions so that any deviation from the norm might be seen as an anomaly. Yet anomalies often have a way of becoming conventions; such was the case in the mid- to late-1970s when a new generation of designers—those schooled in the late sixties and early seventies—began slowly changing the look of book packaging from the traditional big type and little image covers to mini-posters which integrated type and image in the spirit of the late-nineteenth-century advertising posters. Designers such as Fred Marcellino, who at his peak designed over two hundred jackets in one year, and Louise Fili, who as art director of Pantheon Books for ten years developed a distinctive personal vocabulary and publishing house identity, marked the ascendancy of the new style that employed conceptual illustration, abstract photography and collage, subdued colors, and elegantly expressive typography (often hand-lettered reprises of passé forms). While the traditional commercial methods had not (and have not) been eliminated, more artful approaches emerged concurrent with a significant rise in the annual number of books published—and consistent with an increase in the amount of eclectic titles offered to the mass market.

Generations are usually measured in twenty-year intervals, but when referring to generations of designers the period has been compressed into a matter of years. Indeed an even newer generation of book jacket and cover designers has come of age within the past seven years whose work both challenges and compliments the one immediately prior. The style that this generation proffers was first seen in the mid-1980s in trade (or quality) paperback series that featured new, young writers in an economical venue for publishing untested fiction. These new writers' series, which began in the Unites States at Vintage and Penguin, and are dubbed by critics as "yuppiebacks" referring to their targeted audience, were adorned with visual codes designed to capture the new consumers' attention. The paperback equivalent of record albums, yuppiebacks employed Post-modern design conceits—blips, lozenges, and sawtooth rules—and music video imagery—blurry photographs and disjointed visuals—beckoning the young reader to sample the prose within. Pushed even further on the nonfiction books, by art directors Carol Carson and Chip Kidd, this most visible design mannerism today suggests a convergence of pop art (Rauschenberg and Rosenquist), American vernacular (collaged artifacts), computer typography (anamorphic letterforms), and deliberately artless lettering (sometimes excruciatingly tiny titles).

Compared to the conventional "bestseller" jackets and mass market paperbacks, which are often oppressively clichéd, the current style is purposefully abstract, providing only a minimal hint of the content. A fragment here, an icon there, are perhaps pieces in a graphic puzzle that is often never solved, for after the book—or flap copy—is read one still might not find the adequate clues for the imagery. Yet this style still has allure. It suggests newness (or novelty) and hipness. It prompts a second look on the shelves and forces the potential buyer to read the flap (advertising) copy—one of the important steps in hooking the reader. The best of these jackets and covers are intelligent, sophisticated, and witty works of art.

Today stylistic pluralism reigns in book publishing. Actually, more formulas are available for the taking than ever before. But also given the diversity of many publishing programs, untested approaches are not always discouraged. Despite the widespread attempt of marketing experts to influence design decisions, a surprisingly large proportion of the thousands of trade, mass market, scholarly, professional, and educational book jackets and covers produced annually are better designed than ever before—indeed this is a much higher ratio of "good work" than in the magazine field. Hence the yardstick for measuring what is included in this survey of jackets and covers, most designed since 1985 (a period when the change in styles and confluence of methods began), is based first on originality and second on aesthetics. The former does not imply total innovation, though the work of innovative designers is represented, because even they invariably build upon and follow their own efforts—and because innovation is really quite rare. Rather originality imposes a clear vision: not blindly following conventions and clichés. Hence some very contemporary jackets and covers were eliminated in the editing stage simply for slavishly following convention. Aesthetics is much more subjective. How well a particular work stimulates the editors' senses is the single entry requirement. When all the elements, whether old fashioned or progressive, work together then that design (or designs in the case of a series) has succeeded on some fundamental level.

Included in this book are numerous examples by many prolific art directors and designers, underscoring the fact that despite all its pitfalls book publishing is probably the most fertile commercial arena for progressive design today. While selecting the best of a genre invariably obfuscates the problems, nevertheless the quality of the quantity represented here supports the assertion that good graphic design is not just a necessary procedure, but a true virtue.

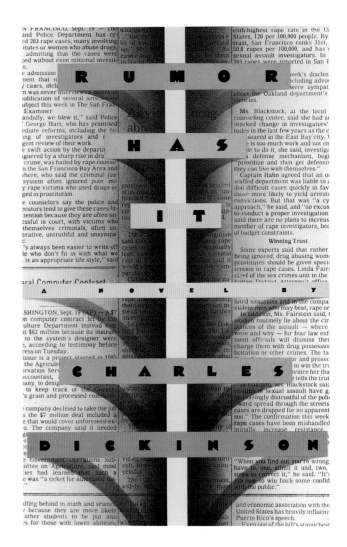

PERFECT GALLOWS
Art Director/Designer: Louise Fili
Illustrator: Robert Goldstrom
Publisher: Pantheon Books

RUMOR HAS IT
Art Director: Linda Kosarin
Designer/Illustrator: Fred Marcellino
Publisher: William Morrow & Co.

ASTROPHOBIA
Art Director: Krystyna Skalski
Designer/Illustrator: Andrzej Dudzinski
Publisher: Grove Weidenfeld

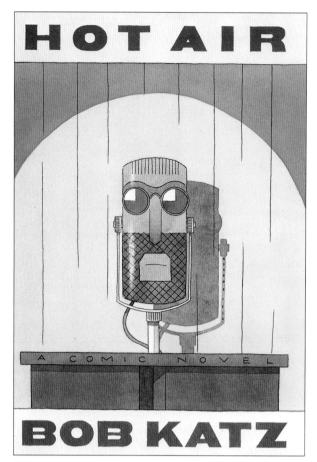

HOT AIR
Art Director: Steven Brower
Designer/Illustrator: Steven Guarnaccia
Publisher: Carol Publishing

BASTARD OUT OF CAROLINA
Art Director: Neil Stuart   Designer: Michael Ian Kaye
Photographer: Dorothea Lange
Publisher: Viking Penguin

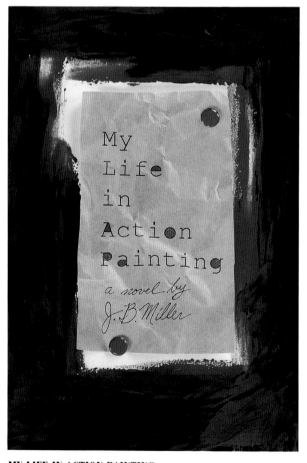

MY LIFE IN ACTION PAINTING
Art Director: Krystyna Skalski
Designer: Marc Cohen
Publisher: Grove Weidenfeld

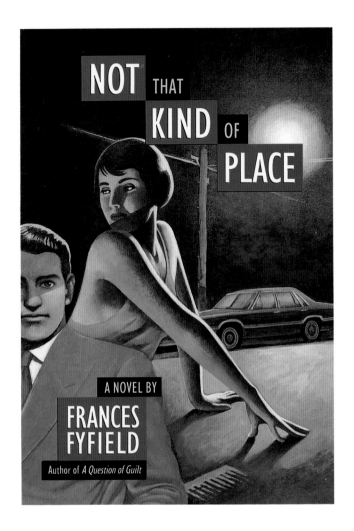

NOT THAT KIND OF PLACE
Art Director: Barbara Buck
Designer/Illustrator: Paul Davis Studio
Publisher: Pocket Books

PENELOPE'S HAT
Art Director: Frank Metz   Designer: Louise Fili
Photographer: Marcia Lippman
Publisher: Simon & Schuster

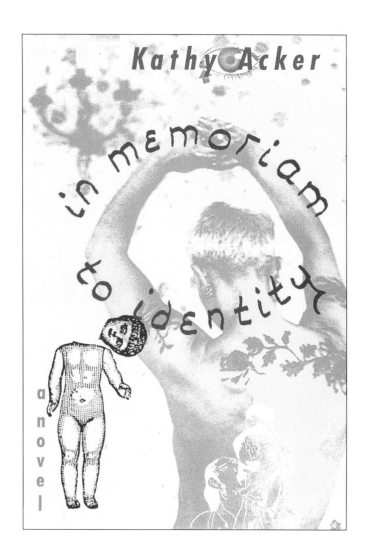

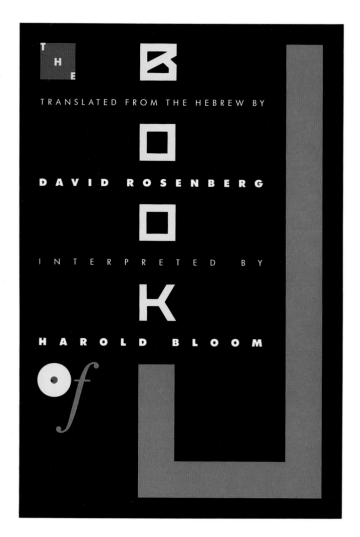

IN MEMORIAM TO IDENTITY
Art Director: Krystyna Skalski   Designer: Jo Bonney
Photographer: Michel Delsol
Publisher: Grove Weidenfeld

THE BOOK OF J
Art Director: Krystyna Skalski
Designer: Carin Goldberg
Publisher: Grove Weidenfeld

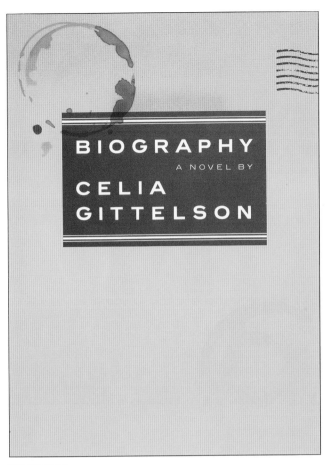

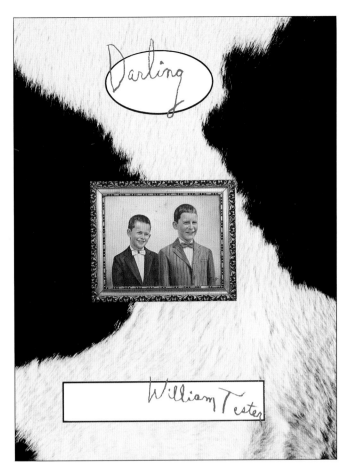

BIOGRAPHY
Art Director: Carol Carson
Designer: Barbara de Wilde
Publisher: Alfred A. Knopf

DARLING
Art Director: Carol Carson
Designer: Chip Kidd
Publisher: Alfred A. Knopf

INFANTA
Art Director: Neil Stuart   Designer: Todd Rodom
Illustrator: Chris Gall
Publisher: Viking Penguin

ACCLAIM FOR *COME SUNDAY*

"*Come Sunday* resists classification. There are affinities with Kafka and with Conrad's *Heart of Darkness*. This is far from the usual semi-autobiographical first novel, groping for meaning and identity, though there are profound insights into identity and the ultimate impasse of control and authority. Morrow draws on an astonishingly wide knowledge and experience of people, places, and history, and puts a rich command of language at the service of his lapidary and mysterious plot. A very engrossing story."
—WILLIAM S. BURROUGHS

"*Come Sunday* is a brilliantly written work of political and mythical grandeur, an important first novel."
—JOHN HAWKES

"A ferociously impressive first novel, risky and ambitious and conversant with a hundred human dialects. Morrow knows that fiction, like sex, is friction, and he's fearless as to the number and nature of the sticks he rubs together. I'm sure that writing *Come Sunday* was a real adventure of the soul for him, for it is precisely that for the reader."
—PETER STRAUB

"A dark, brilliant adventure, American in inspiration and humor, hemispheric in scope.... A moving and fascinating novel."
—JOSEPH MCELROY

"I welcome Bradford Morrow's remarkable first novel, *Come Sunday*. The writing is charged with the menace of a time bomb. History is treated as scenario, commodity, and motivation in this exhilarating, carefully orchestrated book." —WALTER ABISH

"Exciting, passionate, committed, compelling: this is a knockout of a book."
—HARRY MATHEWS

"If only every American first novelist wrote this well and had an imagination so strong. Morrow writes with mellow density and austere finesse. The central situation is both dramatic and exotic, as hard to resist as to exhaust. I was captivated by the sheer display of mind and nourished by the virtuoso style. He deserves applause for this audacious debut."
—PAUL WEST

COME SUNDAY
BRADFORD MORROW

COME SUNDAY
A NOVEL

BRADFORD MORROW

WEIDENFELD & NICOLSON

9 781555 841782
ISBN 1-55584-178-3

COME SUNDAY
Art Director: Krystyna Skalski
Illustrator: José Ortega
Publisher: Weidenfeld & Nicholson

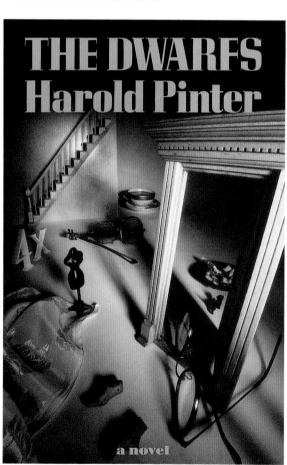

THE DWARFS
Harold Pinter

4X

a novel

THE DWARFS
Art Director/Designer: Krystyna Skalski
Photographer: Michele Clement
Publisher: Grove Weidenfeld

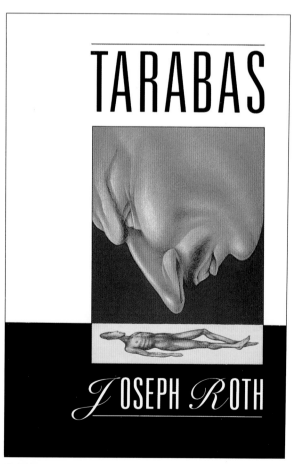

TARABAS

JOSEPH ROTH

TARABAS
Art Director/Designer: Gary Day Ellison
Illustrator: Anita Kunz
Publisher: Picador Books

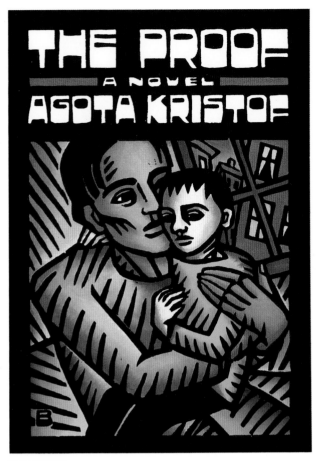

THE PROOF
Art Director: Krystyna Skalski
Designer/Illustrator: Bascove
Publisher: Grove Weidenfeld

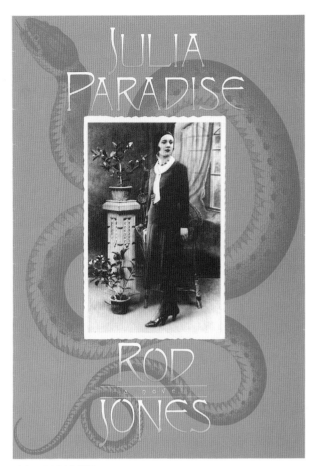

JULIA PARADISE
Art Director: Frank Metz   Designer: Louise Fili
Photography: Bettmann Archive
Publisher: Summit Books

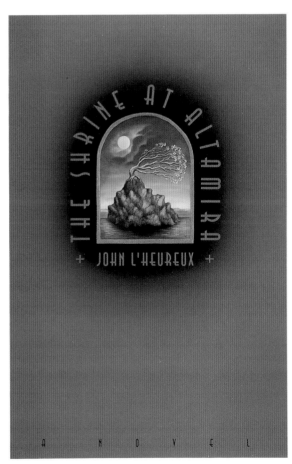

THE SHRINE AT ALTAMIRA
Art Director: Neil Stuart   Designer: Michael Ian Kaye
Illustrator: Anita Kunz
Publisher: Viking Penguin

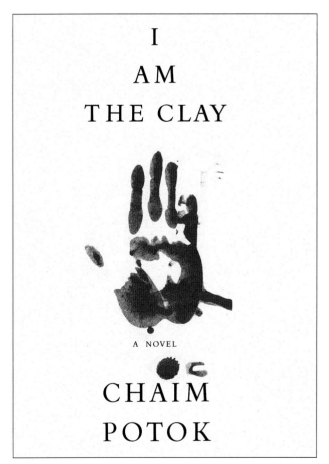

I AM THE CLAY
Art Director: Carol Carson
Designers: Barbara de Wilde and Archie Ferguson
Publisher: Alfred A. Knopf

KILL HOLE
Art Director: Krystyna Skalski
Designer/Illustrator: Bascove
Publisher: Grove Press

SOMETHING LIKE A LOVE AFFAIR
Art Director: Jackie Merri Meyer   Designer: Daniel Pelavin
Illustrator: John Martinez
Publisher: Warner/Mysterious Press

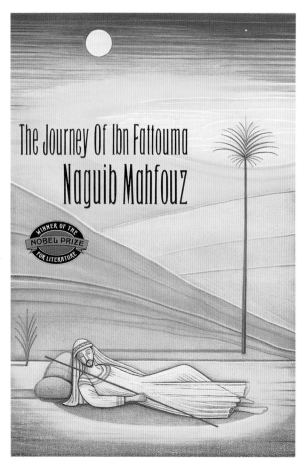

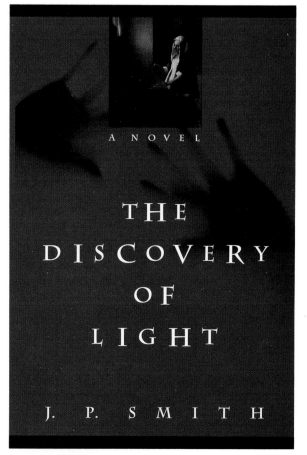

THE JOURNEY OF IBN FATTOUMA
Art Director/Designer: Julie Duquet
Illustrator: Steven Rydberg
Publisher: Doubleday

THE DISCOVERY OF LIGHT
Designer/Photographer: Michael Ian Kaye
Artist: Jan Vermeer
Publisher: Viking Penguin

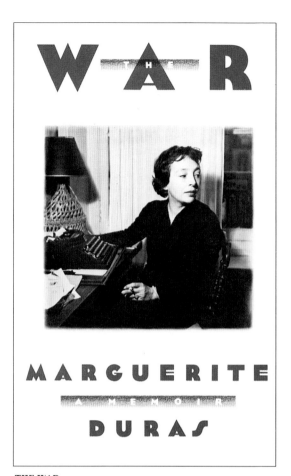

THE TREE OF HANDS
Art Director/Designer: Louise Fili
Illustrator: Anita Kunz
Publisher: Pantheon Books

THE WAR
Art Director/Designer: Louise Fili
Publisher: Pantheon Books

SYLVIA
Art Director/Designer: Steven Brower
Illustrator: Steven Brower
Publisher: Carol Publishing Group

THE SURPRISE OF BURNING
Art Director: Sara Eisenman   Designer: Rita Marshall
Illustrator: Etienne Delessert
Publisher: Alfred A. Knopf

LIGHT
Art Director/Designer: Louise Fili
Artist: Claude Monet
Publisher: Pantheon Books

DEATH IN A SERENE CITY
Art Director: Linda Kosarin
Designer/Illustrator: Fred Marcellino
Publisher: William Morrow & Co.

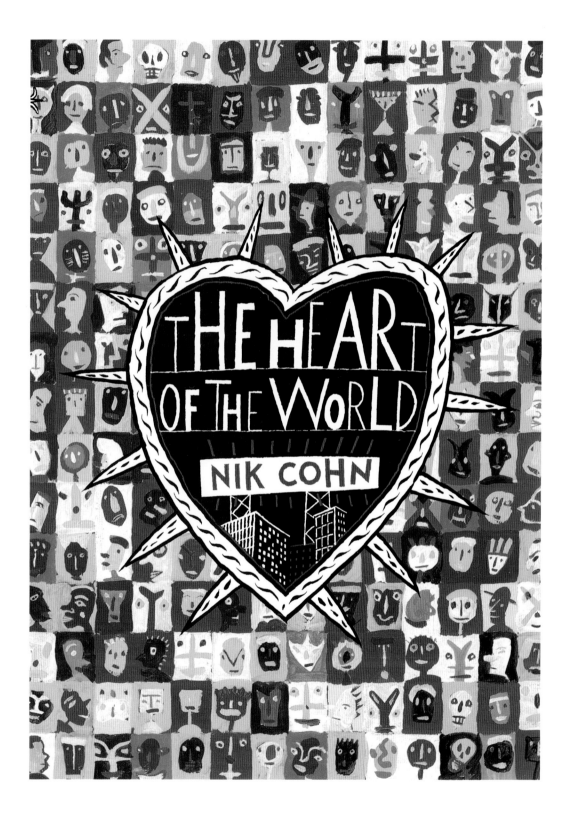

THE HEART OF THE WORLD
Designer/Illustrator: Jeffrey Fisher
Publisher: Chatto & Windus Ltd.

THE LOST FATHER
Art Director: Carol Carson
Designer/Illustrator: Barbara de Wilde
Publisher: Alfred A. Knopf

ARCHIPELAGO
Art Director/Designer: Louise Fili
Illustrator: Robert Goldstrom
Publisher: Pantheon Books

SEXING THE CHERRY
Illustrator: Jeffrey Fisher
Publisher: Bloomsbury Press

"*DREAMING IN CUBAN* IS A MAR-
VELOUS NOVEL AND THE DEBUT OF A
BRILLIANT STORYTELLER. I SUSPECT
WE'LL BE HEARING FROM CRISTINA
GARCIA FOR SOME TIME TO COME—
SHE HAS A GREAT DEAL TO SAY, AND
SHE SAYS IT WONDERFULLY WELL."
—RUSSELL BANKS

ISBN 0-679-40883-5

DREAMING IN CUBAN
Art Director: Carol Carson
Designer: Chip Kidd
Publisher: Alfred A. Knopf

THE ONE WHO SET OUT TO STUDY FEAR
Designer/Illustrator: Jeffrey Fisher
Publisher: Bloomsbury Press

MEXICO DAYS
Art Director: Krystyna Skalski
Designer/Illustrator: José Ortega
Publisher: Weidenfeld & Nicholson

31

DECEPTION
Art Director/Designer: Peter Dyer
Photographer: The Douglas Brothers
Publisher: Jonathan Cape

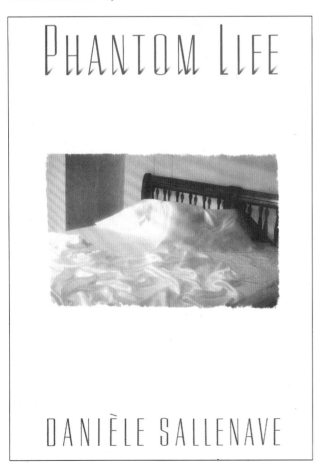

PHANTOM LIFE
Art Director/Designer: Louise Fili
Photographer: Marcia Lippman
Publisher: Pantheon Books

THE REVOLUTION OF LITTLE GIRLS
Art Director: Carol Carson
Designer: Barbara de Wilde
Publisher: Alfred A. Knopf

THE BLINDFOLD
Art Director: Frank Metz   Designer: Carin Goldberg
Photographer: Benno Friedman
Publisher: Poseidon Press

ROOM TEMPERATURE
Designer: Senate Design Ltd.
Publisher: Granta Books

THE MAMBO KINGS PLAY SONGS OF LOVE
Art Director: Dorris Janowitz
Designer/Illustrator: Fred Marcellino
Publisher: Farrar Straus Giroux

ANOTHER PRESENT ERA
Art Director: Dorris Janowitz   Designer: Louise Fili
Artist: Hugh Ferris
Publisher: Farrar Straus Giroux

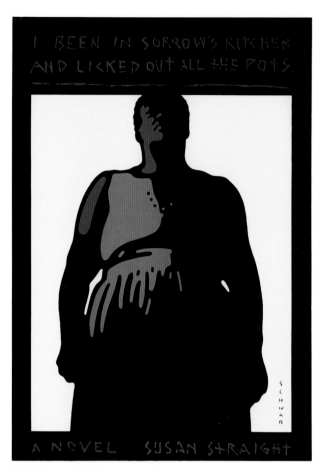

I BEEN IN SORROW'S KITCHEN AND LICKED OUT ALL THE POTS
Art Director: Victor Weaver
Designer/Illustrator: Michael Schwab
Publisher: Hyperion

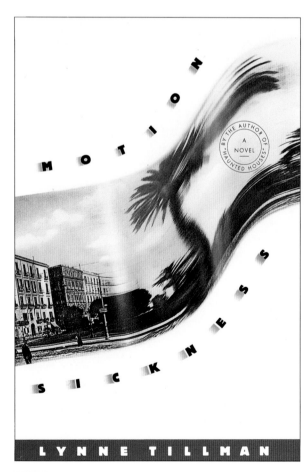

MOTION SICKNESS
Art Director: Frank Metz
Designer: Louise Fili
Publisher: Poseidon Press

DOG DAYS
Art Director: Frank Metz   Designer: Carin Goldberg
Illustrator: Steven Guarnaccia
Publisher: Simon & Schuster

REAL ESTATE
Designer: Paula Scher, Pentagram
Publisher: Simon & Schuster

PEARL'S PROGRESS
Art Director: Carol Carson
Designer/Illustrator: Steven Guarnaccia
Publisher: Alfred A. Knopf

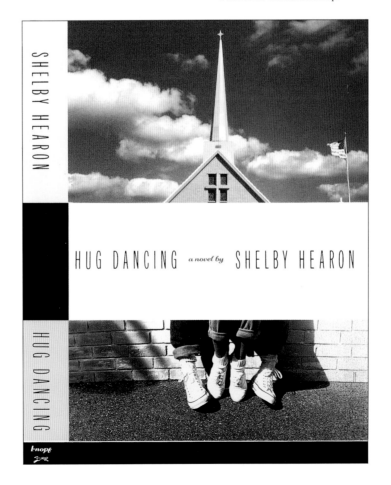

HUG DANCING
Art Director: Carol Carson   Designer: Barbara de Wilde
Photographer: Dan Lloyd Taylor
Publisher: Alfred A. Knopf

THE JUDGMENT DAY ARCHIVES
Art Director: Sharon Smith
Designer/Illustrator: Mark Fox/BlackDog
Publisher: Mercury House

EVER AFTER
Art Director/Designer: Carol Carson
Publisher: Alfred A. Knopf

BREATH OF FREEDOM
Designer: Senate Design Ltd.
Photographer: Michael Heritage
Publisher: Granta Books

KRAZY KAT
Art Director: Sara Eisenman
Designer/Illustrator: Steven Guarnaccia
Publisher: Alfred A. Knopf

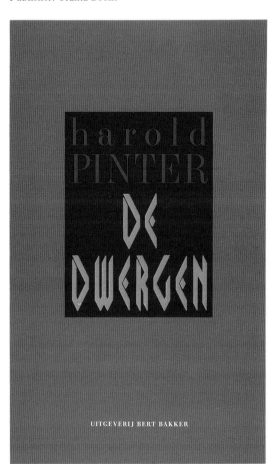

DE DWERGEN
Designer: Rick Vermeulen, Hard Werken Design
Publisher: Uitgeverij Bert Bakker

DEFENDING CIVILIZATION
Art Director: Krystyna Skalski
Designer/Illustrator: Larry Noble
Publisher: Weidenfeld & Nicholson

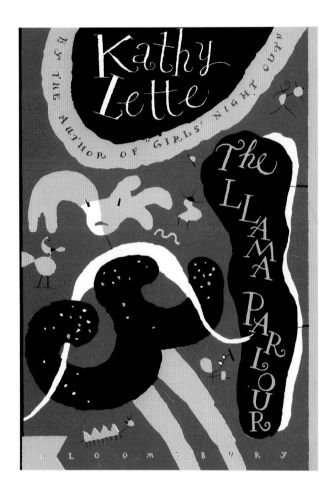

LIKE CHINA
Art Director: Linda Kosarin
Designer/Typographer: Fred Marcellino
Publisher: William Morrow & Co.

THE LLAMA PARLOUR
Designer/Illustrator: Jeffrey Fisher
Publisher: Bloomsbury Press

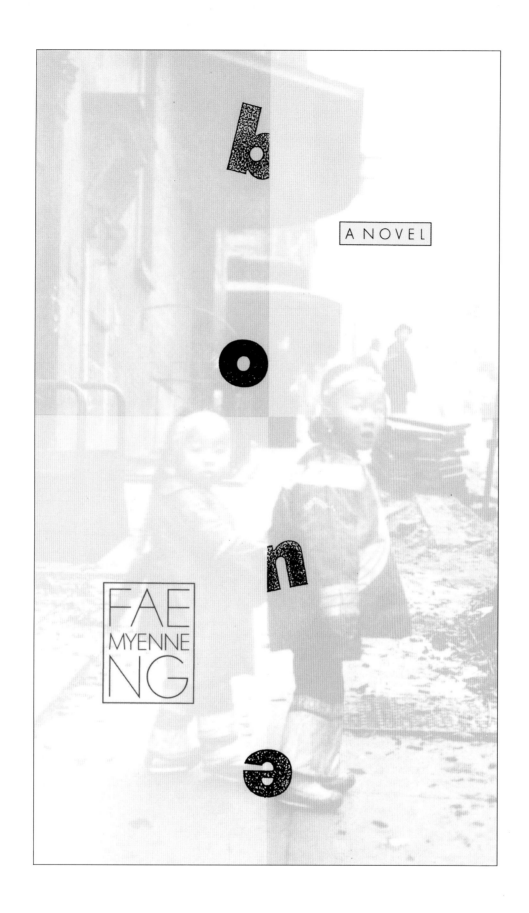

b o n e

A NOVEL

FAE MYENNE NG

BONE
Art Director: Victor Weaver   Designer: Carin Goldberg
Photographer: Genthe
Publisher: Hyperion

IMMORTALITY
Art Director: Krystyna Skalski
Designer/Illustrator: Fred Marcellino
Publisher: Grove Weidenfeld

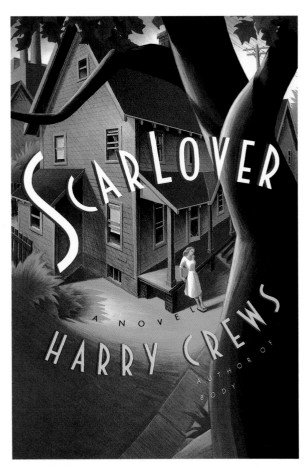

SCAR LOVER
Art Director: Frank Metz   Designer: Jackie Seow
Illustrator: Cathleen Toelke
Publisher: Poseidon Press

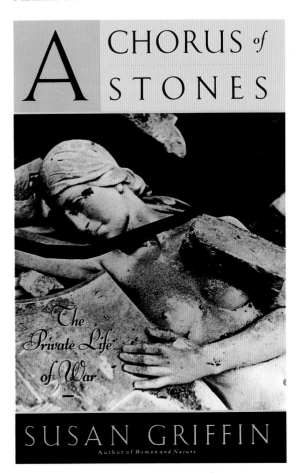

A CHORUS OF STONES
Art Director: Julie Duquet   Designer: Mario Pulice
Photography: Lee Miller Archives
Publisher: Doubleday

SHIRA
Art Director/Designer: Louise Fili
Photographer: Marcia Lippman
Publisher: Schocken Books

THE RUNAWAY SOUL
Art Director: Dorris Janowitz
Designer: Fred Marcellino
Publisher: Farrar Straus Giroux

ASYA
Art Director: Carol Carson   Designer: Archie Ferguson
Photographer: Diana Klein
Publisher: Alfred A. Knopf

ALL THE PRETTY HORSES
Art Director: Carol Carson   Designer: Chip Kidd
Photographer: David Katzenstein
Publisher: Alfred A. Knopf

EMILY L.
Art Director/Designer: Louise Fili
Illustrator: John Martinez
Publisher: Pantheon Books

THE ANGELIC GAME
Designer/Illustrator: Jeffrey Fisher
Publisher: Bloomsbury Press

THE TAX INSPECTOR
Art Director: Carol Carson
Designer: Chip Kidd
Publisher: Alfred A. Knopf

TRIBES
Art Director/Designer: Julie Duquet
Photographer: Barry Marcus
Publisher: Doubleday

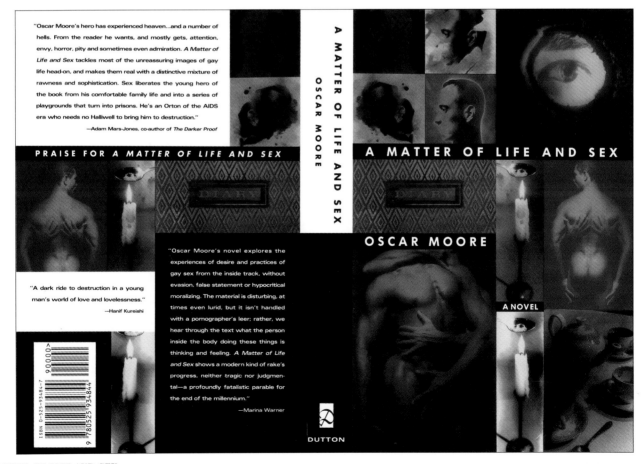

A MATTER OF LIFE AND SEX
Art Director: Neil Stuart   Designer: Michael Ian Kaye
Photographer: Amy Guip
Publisher: Viking Penguin

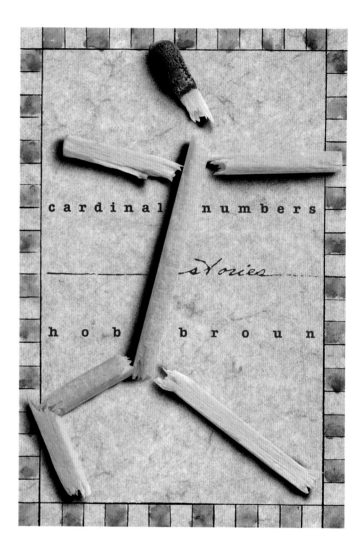

BETTER GET YOUR ANGEL ON
Art Director: Carol Carson
Designers: Barbara de Wilde and Chip Kidd
Publisher: Alfred A. Knopf

CARDINAL NUMBERS
Art Director: Sara Eisenman
Designer/Illustrator: Marc Cohen
Publisher: Alfred A. Knopf

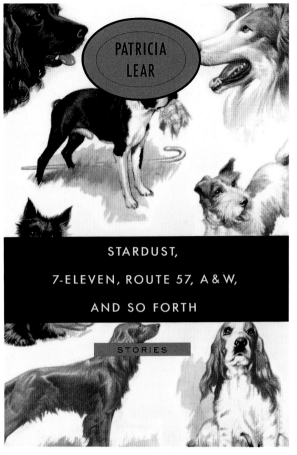

STARDUST, 7-ELEVEN, ROUTE 57, A&W, AND SO FORTH
Art Director/Designer: Carol Carson
Publisher: Alfred A. Knopf

TALKING TO THE DEAD
Art Director/Designer: Julie Duquet
Illustrator: Steven Rydberg
Publisher: Doubleday

CITY OF BOYS
Art Director/Designer: Peter Dyer
Photographer: Bruce Davidson/Magnum
Publisher: Jonathan Cape

As Much As I Know SUSAN THAMES

As Much As I Know SUSAN THAMES

STORIES

Random House

AS MUCH AS I KNOW
Art Director: Andy Carpenter
Designer: Barbara de Wilde
Publisher: Random House

PANGS OF LOVE
Art Director: Carol Carson
Designer: Barbara de Wilde
Publisher: Alfred A. Knopf

PARTICULARLY CATS...AND RUFUS
Art Director: Carol Carson
Designer/Illustrator: James McMullan
Publisher: Alfred A. Knopf

ORANGES FROM SPAIN
Art Director/Designer: Peter Dyer
Photographer: Gilles Peress/Magnum
Publisher: Jonathan Cape

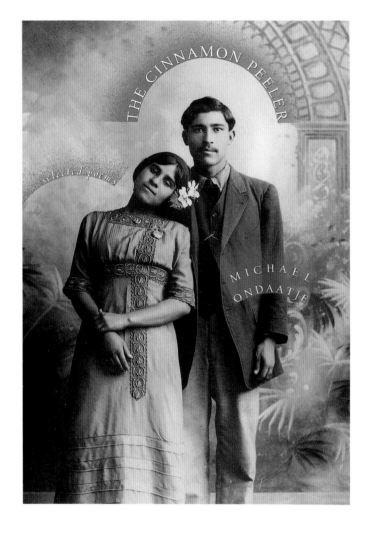

LATE AND POSTHUMOUS POEMS
Art Director: Krystyna Skalski
Designer/Illustrator: Daniel Pelavin
Publisher: Grove Press

THE CINNAMON PEELER
Art Director: Carol Carson   Designer: Archie Ferguson
Photography: Archivo Romualso Garcia
Publisher: Alfred A. Knopf

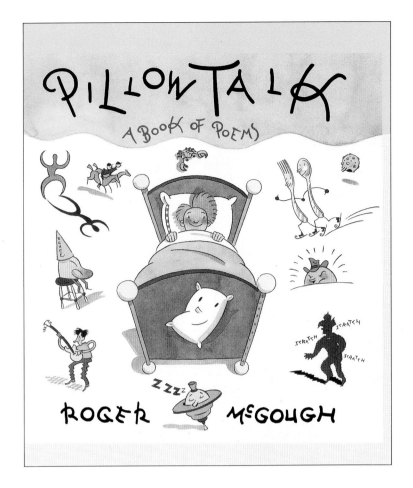

PILLOW TALK
Art Director: Ronnie Wilkins
Designer/Illustrator: Steven Guarnaccia
Publisher: Viking Penguin

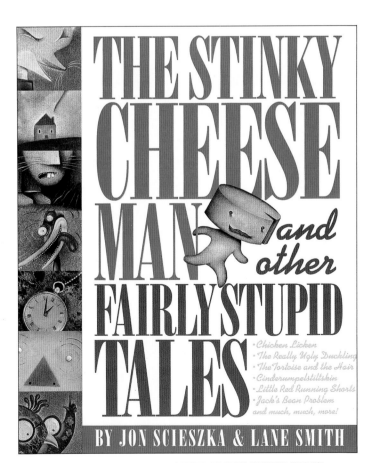

THE STINKY CHEESE MAN AND OTHER FAIRLY STUPID TALES
Art Director: Neil Stuart   Designer: Molly Leach
Illustrator: Lane Smith
Publisher: Viking Penguin

THE LEGEND OF SLEEPY HOLLOW
Art Director/Designer: Rita Marshall
Illustrator: Gary Kelley
Publisher: Stewart, Tabori & Chang/Creative Education

THE ORANGE BOOK
Designer/Illustrator: Richard McGuire
Publisher: Rizzoli International Publications

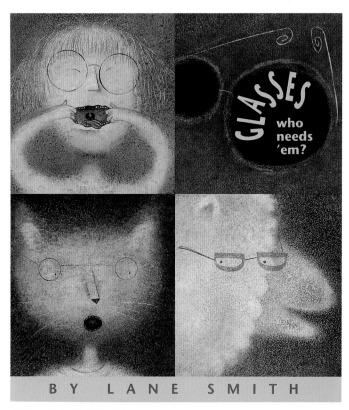

GLASSES, WHO NEEDS 'EM?
Art Director: Neil Stuart   Designer: Molly Leach
Illustrator: Lane Smith
Publisher: Viking Penguin

THE BIG PETS
Art Director: Neil Stuart
Illustrator: Lane Smith
Publisher: Viking Penguin

Illustrations by Etienne Delessert. Story by Rita Marshall

I Hate to Read!

All children like to read stories. The love of "the story," in some form or other, is indeed a characteristic of the human mind, and exists everywhere, in all con- ditions of life. But stories are the sweets of our mental existence, and only a few of the best and greatest have in them the ele- ments which will lead to a strong and vigor- ous mind- growth. Constant feeding upon light literature —however good that literature may be in itself— will debilitate and corrupt the men- tal appetite of the child, much the same as an un- restrained indul- gence in jam and preserves will under mine and destroy his physi- cal health. In either case, if no result more serious occurs, the worst forms of dyspepsia will follow.

I HATE TO READ!
Art Director/Designer: Rita Marshall
Illustrator: Etienne Delessert
Publisher: Creative Education

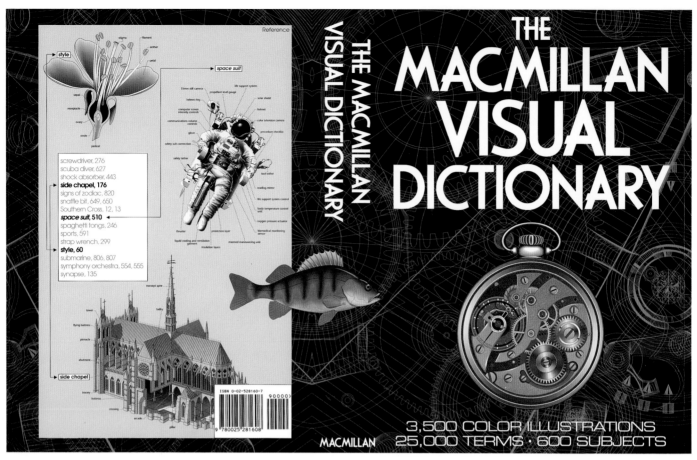

THE MACMILLAN VISUAL DICTIONARY
Art Director/Designer: Susan Newman
Illustrator: Computer generated
Publisher: Macmillan Publishing Co.

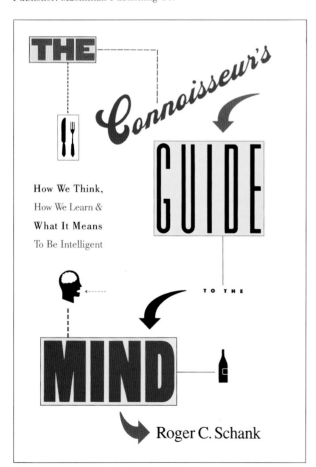

THE CONNOISSEUR'S GUIDE TO THE MIND
Art Director: Frank Metz
Designer: Carin Goldberg
Publisher: Summit Books

SLOW FOOD
Art Director/Designer: Jackie Merri Meyer
Illustrator: Douglas Smith
Publisher: Warner Books

TRICK OR TREAT
Art Director: Howard Klein
Designer: Alexander Isley
Publisher: Clarkson Potter

THE INSANITY OF NORMALITY
Art Director: Krystyna Skalski
Designer: Carin Goldberg
Publisher: Grove Weidenfeld

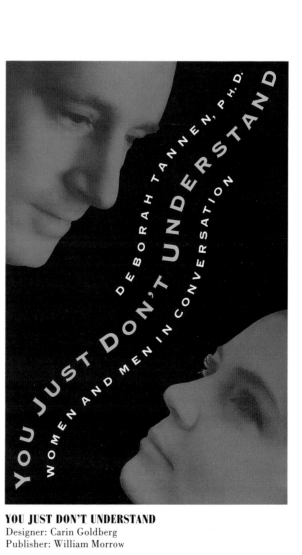

YOU JUST DON'T UNDERSTAND
Designer: Carin Goldberg
Publisher: William Morrow

53

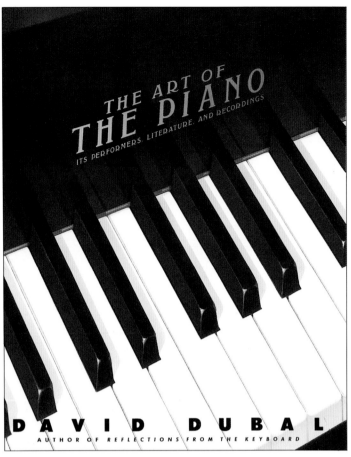

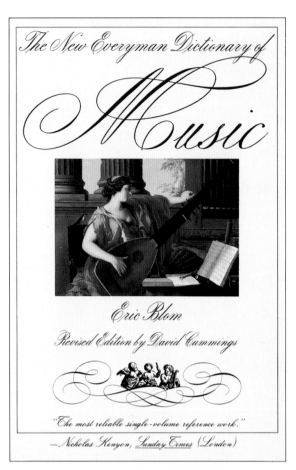

THE ART OF THE PIANO
Art Director: Frank Metz
Designer: Fred Marcellino
Publisher: Summit Books

THE NEW EVERYMAN DICTIONARY OF MUSIC
Art Director: Krystyna Skalski   Designer: Louise Fili
Artist: Laurent de Lattire
Publisher: Grove Weidenfeld

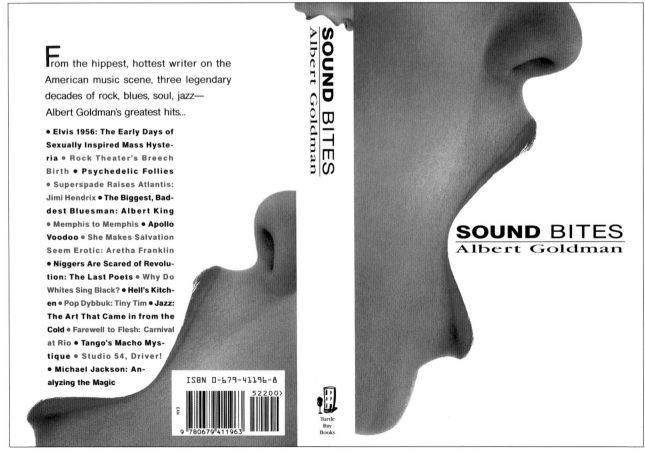

SOUND BITES
Art Director: Charles Woods   Designer: Mark Balet
Photographer: Raymond Meier
Publisher: Turtle Bay Books

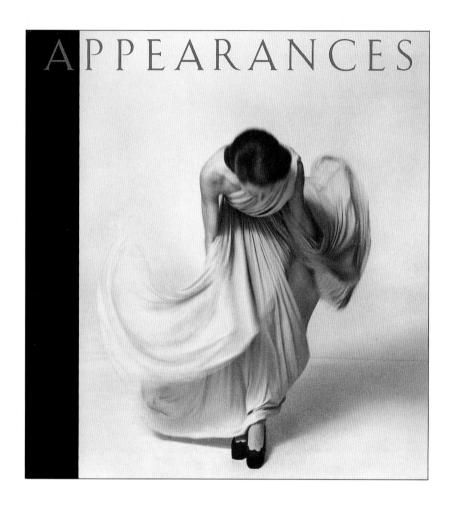

APPEARANCES
Art Director/Designer: Peter Dyer
Photographer: Louis Faurer
Publisher: Jonathan Cape

ART OF THE THIRD REICH
Art Director: Samuel N. Antupit   Designer: Robert McKee
Artist: Ludwig Hohlwein
Publisher: Harry N. Abrams

ARCHITECTS OF FORTUNE
Art Director: Krystyna Skalski
Designer: Carin Goldberg
Publisher: Weidenfeld and Nicholson

ALEX KATZ NIGHT PAINTINGS
Art Director/Designer: Samuel N. Antupit
Artist: Alex Katz
Publisher: Harry N. Abrams

THE NEW URBAN LANDSCAPE
Art Director: Stephen Doyle, Drenttel Doyle Partners
Designer: Andrew Gray   Photography: Courtesy of Con Edison
Publisher: Olympia & York

AMERICAN ILLUSTRATION 10
Designer: Michael Mabry
Illustrator: Gary Baseman
Publisher: Watson Guptill

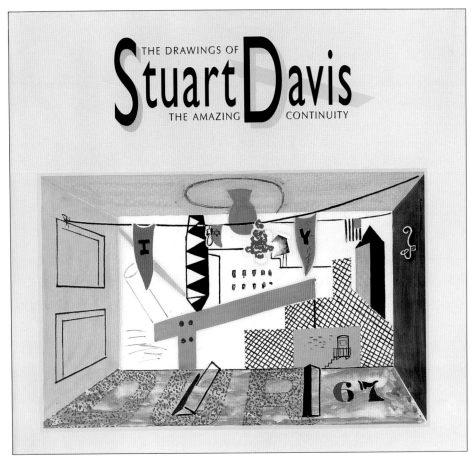

THE DRAWINGS OF STUART DAVIS
Art Director: Samuel N. Antupit   Designer: Robert McKee
Artist: Stuart Davis
Publisher: Harry N. Abrams

Love for sale

The Words and Pictures of Barbara Kruger

Text by Kate Linker

LOVE FOR SALE
Art Director/Designer: Samuel N. Antupit
Designer/Illustrator: Barbara Kruger
Publisher: Harry N. Abrams

GRAPHIC STYLE: FROM VICTORIAN TO POSTMODERN
Designer/Illustrator: Seymour Chwast
Publisher: Harry N. Abrams

ADWEEK PORTFOLIO CREATIVE SERVICES DIRECTORY
Designers: Walter Bernard and Milton Glaser, WBMG Inc.
Photographer: Matthew Klein
Publisher: A/S/M Publications Inc.

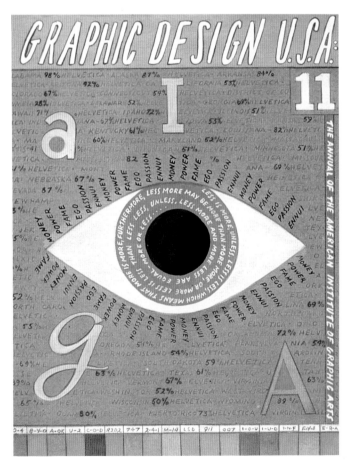

GRAPHIC DESIGN U.S.A.
Designer/Illustrator: Paula Scher
Publisher: Watson Guptil

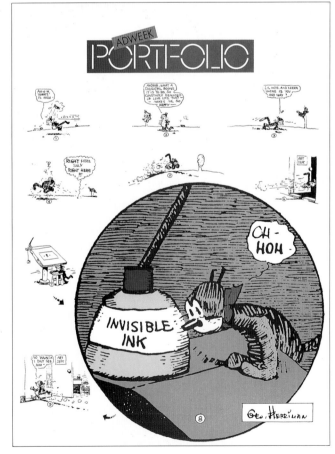

ADWEEK PORTFOLIO
Designers: Walter Bernard and Milton Glaser, WBMG Inc.
Illustrator: George Herriman
Publisher: A/S/M Communications Inc.

TRADEMARKS OF THE '40s AND '50s
Designer: Michael Doret
Publisher: Chronicle Books

CHARACTER TRADEMARKS
Designer: John Mendenhall
Publisher: Chronicle Books

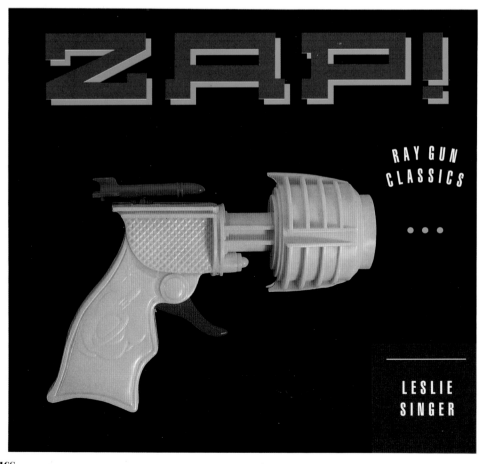

ZAP! RAY GUN CLASSICS
Art Director: Karen Pike   Designer: Karen Smidth
Photographer: Dixie Knight
Publisher: Chronicle Books

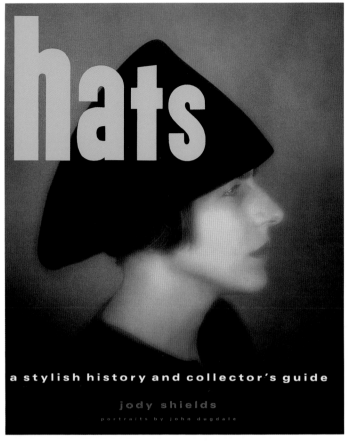

HATS
Art Director: Howard Klein   Designer: Helene Silverman
Photographer: John Dugdale
Publisher: Clarkson Potter

CHAIR
Designer: Peter Bradford
Publisher: T.Y. Crowell, New York

FABULOUS FABRICS OF THE 50s
Art Director: Michael Carabetta   Designer: Michele Wethebee
Photographer: Bruce Beaton
Publisher: Chronicle Books

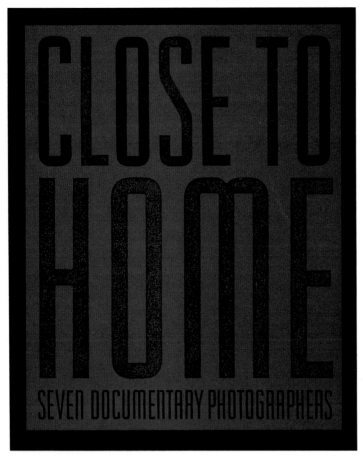

CLOSE TO HOME
Designer: Michael Mabry
Publisher: The Friends of Photography

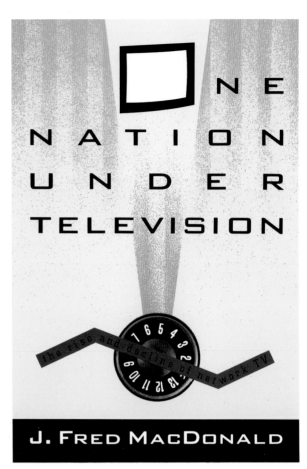

ONE NATION UNDER TELEVISION
Art Director: Marge Anderson
Designer: Archie Ferguson
Publisher: Pantheon Books

HELLO, I MUST BE GOING
Art Director/Designer: Steven Brower
Publisher: Carol Publishing Group

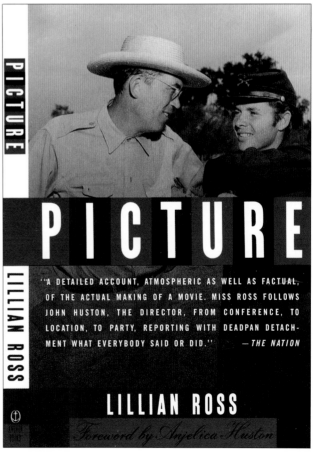

PICTURE
Art Director: Julie Duquet   Designer: Carol Carson
Photographer: Photofest
Publisher: Doubleday/Anchor Books

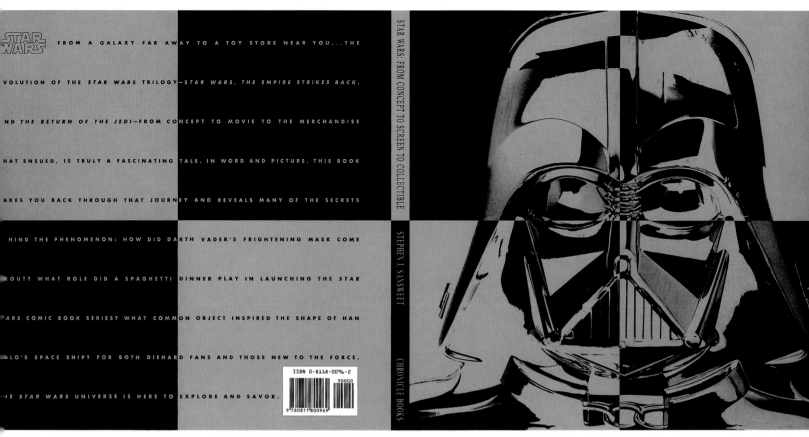

STAR WARS: FROM CONCEPT TO SCREEN TO COLLECTIBLE
Art Director: Michael Carabetta
Designers: Earl Gee and Fani Chung
Publisher: Chronicle Books

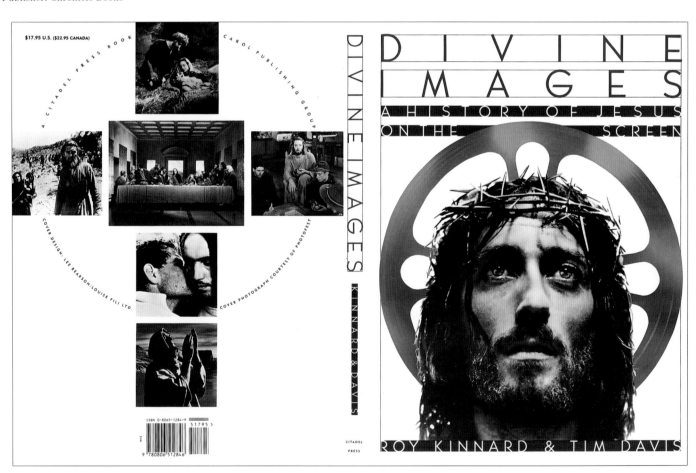

DIVINE IMAGES: A HISTORY OF JESUS ON THE SCREEN
Art Director: Steve Brower   Designers: Lee Bearson and Louise Fili
Photographer: Photofest
Publisher: Citadel Press/Carol Publishing Group

COOKING CARIBE
Art Director: Howard Klein   Designer: Elizabeth Van Itallie
Illustrator: Paula Munck
Publisher: Clarkson Potter

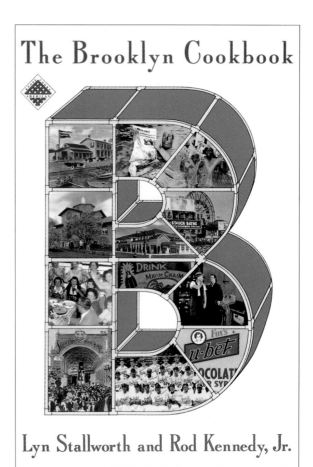

THE BROOKLYN COOKBOOK
Designer/Illustrator: Stephanie Tevonian
Publisher: Alfred A. Knopf

PARIS BISTRO COOKING
Art Director: Howard Klein   Designer: Louise Fili
Photographer: Guy Bouchet
Publisher: Clarkson Potter

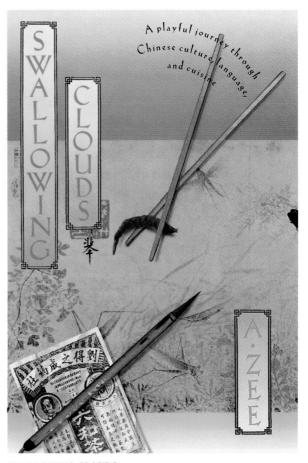

SWALLOWING CLOUDS
Art Director: Frank Metz
Designer: Louise Fili
Publisher: Simon & Schuster

ADVANCE PRAISE FOR *PEPPERS*

AMAL NAJ

Peppers

AMAL NAJ

Peppers

Knopf

A STORY OF HOT PURSUITS

"A tasty piece of eccentricity: through his unprepossessing subject, Naj unfolds history, economics, psychology and law, showing us a whole world in a grain of pepper."

—Pico Iyer

"As a chile aficionado, I couldn't put this book down. It contains fascinating new aspects of chile lore, and I found myself learning something new in every chapter. If you weren't a chile lover before, this book will certainly convert you. The well-written tales alone take the noble chile out of obscurity and into the forefront of the culinary scene."

—Mark Miller

ISBN 0-394-57077-4

PEPPERS
Art Director: Carol Carson
Designer: Chip Kidd
Publisher: Alfred A. Knopf

THE INTERNATIONAL CHOCOLATE COOKBOOK
Art Director: Jim Wageman
Designer: Rita Marshall Photographer: Martin Jacobs
Publisher: Stewart, Tabori & Chang

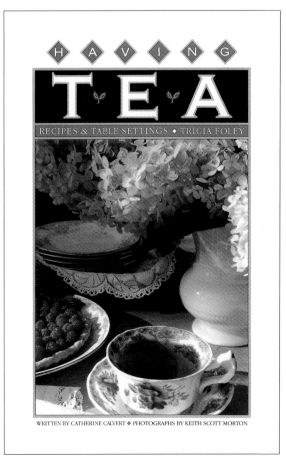

HAVING TEA
RECIPES & TABLE SETTINGS • TRICIA FOLEY

WRITTEN BY CATHERINE CALVERT ◆ PHOTOGRAPHS BY KEITH SCOTT MORTON

HAVING TEA
Art Director: Gail Towey   Designer: Rita Marshall
Photographer/Illustrator: Keith Scott Morton
Publisher: Clarkson Potter

THE AMERICAN REPLACEMENT OF NATURE
Art Director: Peter R. Kruzan
Designers: Chip Kidd and Barbara de Wilde
Publisher: Currency/Doubleday

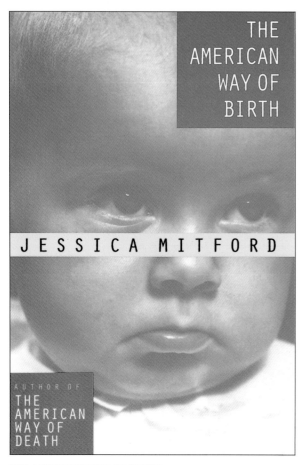

THE AMERICAN WAY OF BIRTH
Art Director/Designer: Neil Stuart
Publisher: Dutton/Penguin Books USA

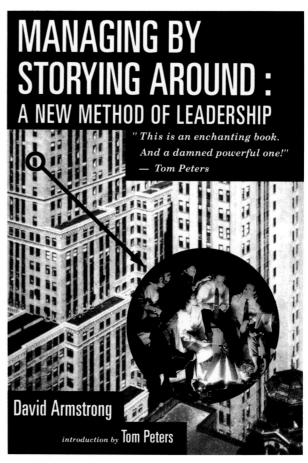

MANAGING BY STORYING AROUND
Art Director: Peter R. Kruzan   Designer: Slatoff & Cohen
Photographer: Joel Brodsky
Publisher: Currency/Doubleday

ff

TERROR

Conor Gearty

TERROR
Art Director: John McConnell, Pentagram
Designers: John McConnell and Jason Godfrey   Photographer: Peter Marlowe, Magnum
Publisher: Faber and Faber

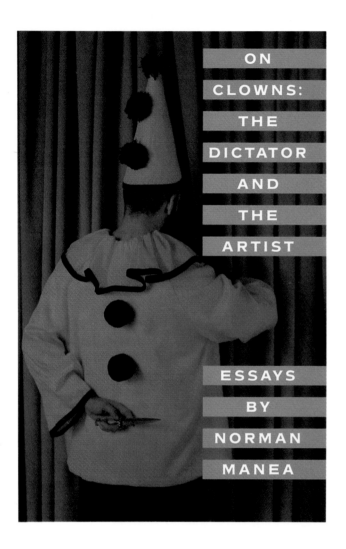

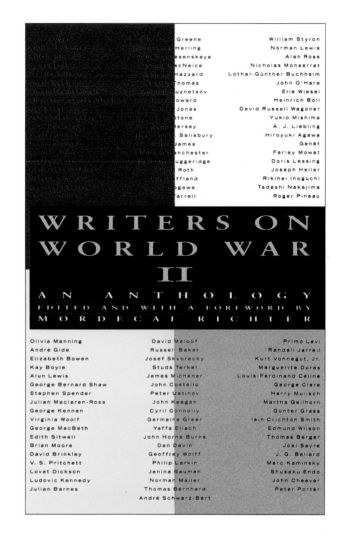

ON CLOWNS: THE DICTATOR AND THE ARTIST
Art Director/Designer: Krystyna Skalski
Photographer: Geof Kern
Publisher: Grove Weidenfeld

WRITERS ON WORLD WAR II
Art Director: Carol Carson
Designer: Archie Ferguson
Publisher: Alfred A. Knopf

IN SEARCH OF LOST ROSES
Art Director: Frank Metz
Designer: Louise Fili
Publisher: Summit Books

FATHERS AND SONS
Art Director: Krystyna Skalski   Designer: Paul Gamarello
Photographer: Marjorie Collins
Publisher: Grove Weidenfeld

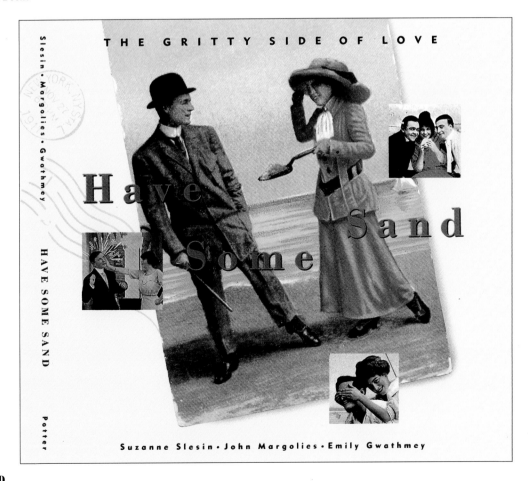

HAVE SOME SAND
Art Director: Howard Klein
Designer: Adriane Stark
Publisher: Clarkson Potter

MADAME DU BARRY
Art Director: Krystyna Skalski   Designer: Louise Fili
Artist: François-Hubert Drouais, 1770
Publisher: Grove Weidenfeld

BLOOD MEMORY
Art Director: Peter R. Kruzan   Designer: Mario J. Pulice
Photographer: Soichi Sunami
Publisher: Doubleday

LOUISE BROOKS
Art Director: Carol Carson   Designer: Louise Fili
Photographer: E.R. Richee
Publisher: Alfred A. Knopf

WANDERING GHOST
Art Director/Designer: Carol Carson
Photography: Lafcadio Hearn Collection
Publisher: Alfred A. Knopf

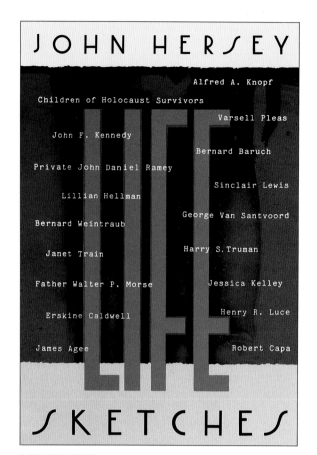

DEAD ELVIS
Art Director/Designer: Julie Duquet
Illustrator/Typographer: Craig DeCamp
Publisher: Doubleday

LIFE SKETCHES
Art Director: Carol Carson
Designer: Archie Ferguson
Publisher: Alfred A. Knopf

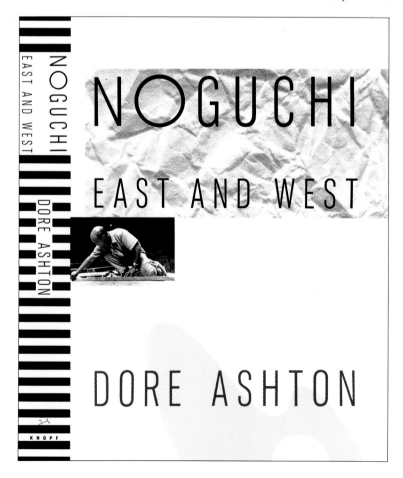

NOGUCHI: EAST AND WEST
Art Director: Carol Carson   Designer: Barbara de Wilde
Photographer: Arthur Lavine
Publisher: Alfred A. Knopf

COME FROM AWAY
Art Director: Frank Metz
Designer/Illustrator: James Steinberg
Publisher: Poseidon Press

TIME AMONG THE MAYA
Art Director: Krystyna Skalski   Designer: Margaret Martinez
Illustrator: John Martinez
Publisher: Weidenfeld and Nicholson

COUSINS
Art Director: Carol Carson   Designer: Archie Ferguson
Photographers: *(front)* Michael Horner, *(back)* Jim Johnson, *(collage)* Geoff Spear
Publisher: Alfred A. Knopf

PAPERBACK

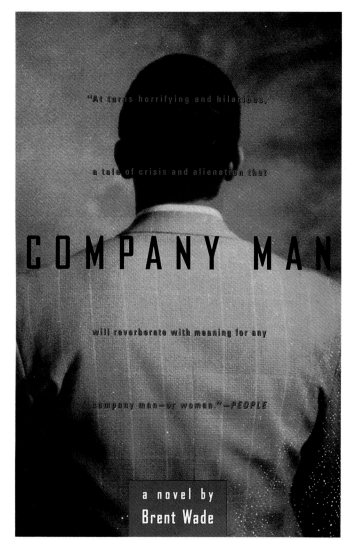

WINGING IT
Designer/Illustrator/Typographer: Sara Schwartz
Publisher: Serpent's Tail

COMPANY MAN
Art Director: Julie Duquet   Designer: iT Design
Photographer: Barry Marcus
Publisher: Doubleday/Anchor Books

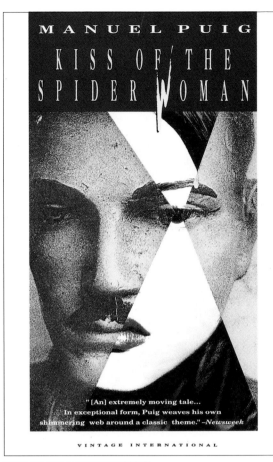

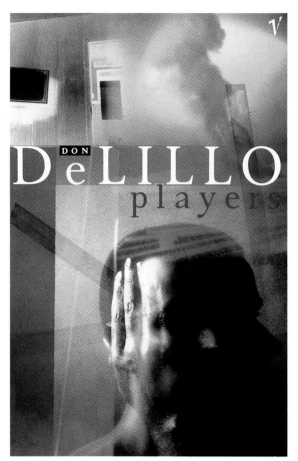

KISS OF THE SPIDER WOMAN
Art Director: Susan Mitchell   Designer: Marc Cohen
Photographers: Carl Rosenstein and David Waldorf
Publisher: Vintage Books

PLAYERS
Designer: Peter Dyer
Photographer: The Douglas Brothers
Publisher: Vintage UK

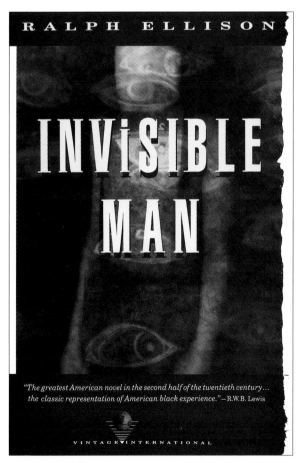

THE THEORY OF EVERYTHING
Art Director: Jackie Merri Meyer
Designer: Julia Kushnirsky   Illustrator: Terry Miura
Publisher: Warner Books

INVISIBLE MAN
Art Director: Susan Mitchell   Designer: Marc Cohen
Photographer: Alesia Exum
Publisher: Vintage Books

A QUESTION OF GUILT
Art Director: Barbara Buck
Designer/Illustrator: Paul Davis Studio
Publisher: Pocket Books

GERECHT
Designer: Rick Vermeulen, Hard Werken Design
Photographer: Jaques Poiesz
Publisher: Uitgeverij Bert Bakker

THE GLASS BEES
Art Director: Stephen Doyle, Drenttel Doyle Partners
Designer: Rosemarie Turk   Artist: Robert Rauschenberg
Publisher: The Noonday Press

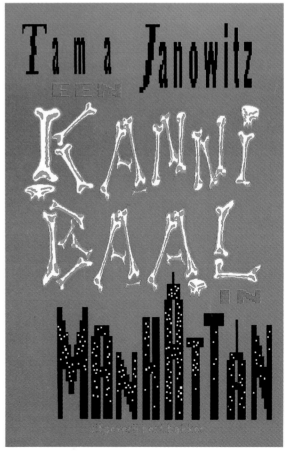

EEN KANNIBAAL IN MANHATTAN
Designer/Typographer: Gerard Hadders, Hard Werken Design
Publisher: Uitgeverij Bert Baker

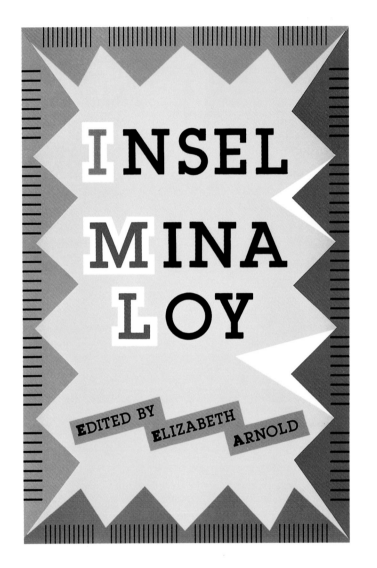

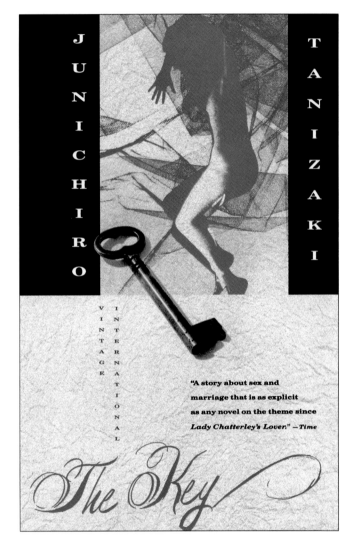

INSEL
Art Director/Designer: Barbara Martin
Publisher: Black Sparrow Press

THE KEY
Art Director: Susan Mitchell   Designer: Marc Cohen
Photographer: Didier Quentin-Dagoise
Publisher: Vintage Books

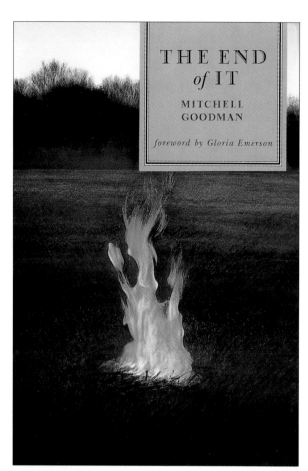

WINTER
Art Director: Sara Eisenman   Designer/Typographer: Jon Valk
Illustrator: John Rush
Publisher: Alfred A. Knopf

THE END OF IT
Designer: Andrew Gray, Drenttel Doyle Partners
Illustrator: Gottfried Helnwein
Publisher: The Noonday Press

WITNESS TO THE FUTURE
Art Director/Designer: Art Chantry
Publisher: Fjord Press

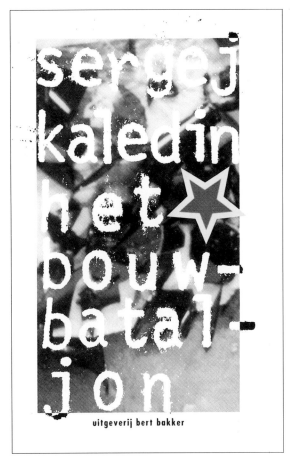

HET BOUWBATELJON
Designer: Hard Werken Design
Illustrator: Maurice Blok
Publisher: Uitgeverij Bert Bakker

JOHNNY GOT HIS GUN
Art Director: Steven Brower
Designer: James Victore
Publisher: Carol Publishing Group

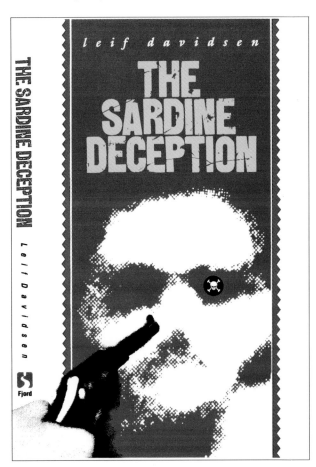

THE SARDINE DECEPTION
Art Director/Designer: Art Chantry
Publisher: Fjord Press

BANDEN
Designer: Rick Vermeulen, Hard Werken Design
Photographer: Peter Vandermeer
Publisher: Uitgeverij Bert Bakker

A BRIEF HISTORY OF CAMOUFLAGE
Art Director/Designer: Barbara Martin
Publisher: Black Sparrow Press

THE FIFTH SON
Art Director: Jackie Merri Meyer   Designer: Wendell Minor
Illustrator: Anthony Russo
Publisher: Warner Books

SPECIAL BRANCH
Designer/Illustrator: Joost Swarte
Publisher: Gaberbocchus Press/De Harmonie

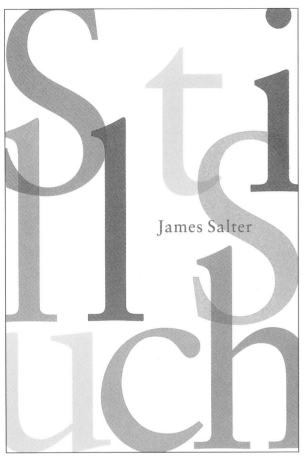

STILL SUCH
Art Director/Designer: Stephen Doyle
Publisher: William Drenttel, New York

PARLOR GAMES
Art Director: Frank Metz   Designer: Carin Goldberg
Illustrator: Steven Guarnaccia
Publisher: Simon & Schuster

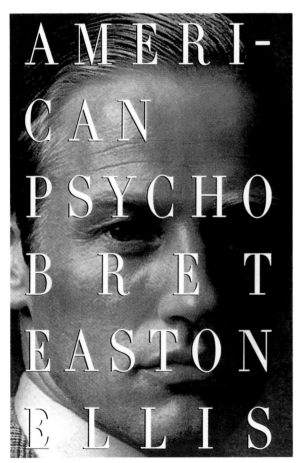

AMERICAN PSYCHO
Art Director: Susan Mitchell   Designer: Lloyd Ziff
Photographer: Robert Erdmann
Publisher: Vintage Books

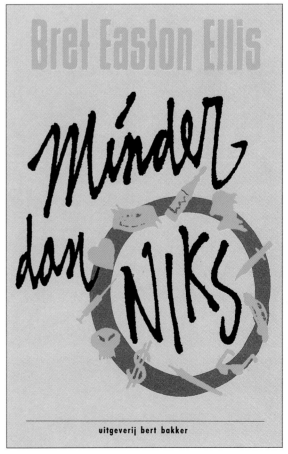

MINDER DAN NIKS
Designer: Rick Vermeulen, Hard Werken Design
Publisher: Uitgeverij Bert Bakker

CAIN'S BOOK
Art Director: Krystyna Skalski
Designer/Illustrator: Josh Gosfield
Publisher: Grove Press

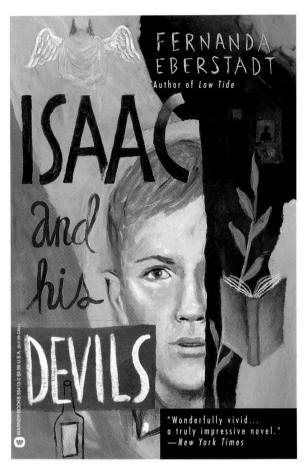

ISAAC AND HIS DEVILS
Art Director: Jackie Merri Meyer
Designer/Illustrator: Josh Gosfield
Publisher: Warner Books

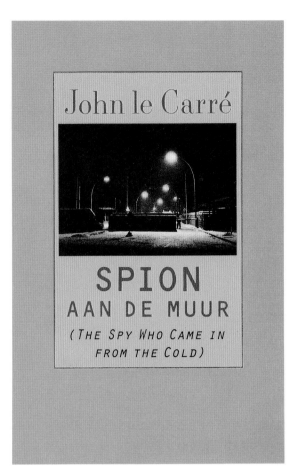

SPION AAN DE MUUR
Designer: Rick Vermeulen, Hard Werken Design
Publisher: Luitingh-Sijthoff

ALLES WARM
Art Director/Designer: Joost Swarte
Illustrator: Joost Swarte
Publisher: Bzztôh

JOE
Art Director: Jackie Merri Meyer   Designer: Louise Fili
Illustrator: Anthony Russo
Publisher: Warner Books

WOMEN OF SAND AND MYRRH
Art Director: Julie Duquet
Designer: Carol Carson
Publisher: Doubleday/Anchor Books

HET KIND VAN DE PRESIDENT
Designer: Gerard Hadders, Hard Werken Design
Photographer: Tom van den Haspel
Publisher: Uitgeverij Bert Bakker

GEKORTWIEKT
Designer: Rick Vermeulen, Hard Werken Design
Photographer: Hans de Jong
Publisher: Uitgeverij Bert Bakker

KINDEREN VAN DE ALBATROS
Designer/Photographer: Gerard Hadders, Hard Werken Design
Publisher: Uitgeverij Bert Bakker

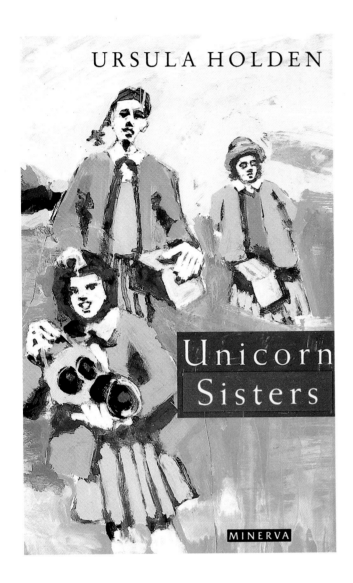

UNICORN SISTERS
Designer: Chris Shamwana
Illustrator: Nick Higgins
Publisher: Minerva

TRASH
Art Director: Patricia Edwards   Designer: Caz Hildebrand
Illustrator: Nick Higgins
Publisher: Penguin UK

A MAN JUMPS OUT OF AN AIRPLANE
Art Director: Howard Klein
Designer/Photographer: Jane Treuhaft
Publisher: Clarkson Potter

HEAD OF A SAD ANGEL
Art Director/Designer: Barbara Martin
Illustrator: Barbara Martin
Publisher: Black Sparrow Press

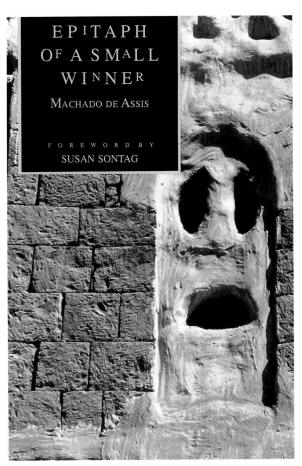

EPITAPH OF A SMALL WINNER
Designer: Stephen Doyle, Drenttel Doyle Partners
Publisher: The Noonday Press

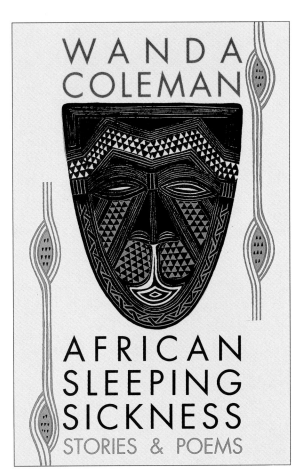

AFRICAN SLEEPING SICKNESS
Art Director/Designer: Barbara Martin
Illustrator: Barbara Martin
Publisher: Black Sparrow Press

HOMESICK
Art Director/Designer: Barbara Martin
Illustrator: Barbara Martin
Publisher: Black Sparrow Press

CHRISTOPHER DURANG EXPLAINS IT ALL FOR YOU
Art Director: Krystyna Skalski   Designer: Jo Bonney
Photographer: Susan Johann
Publisher: Grove Weidenfeld

THE LAST NIGHT OF THE EARTH POEMS
Art Director/Designer: Barbara Martin
Illustrator: Barbara Martin
Publisher: Black Sparrow Press

THE TRICK
Art Director/Designer: Barbara Martin
Publisher: Black Sparrow Press

CULTUUR & TECHNIEK
Designer/Illustrator: Joost Swarte
Publisher: De Harmonie/Het Raadsel

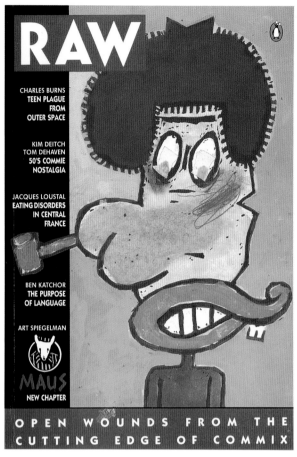

RAW
Art Directors: Art Spiegelman and Francoise Mouly
Illustrator: Gary Panter
Publisher: Penguin

NIET ZO, MAAR ZO!
Designer/Illustrator: Joost Swarte
Publisher: De Harmonie/Het Raadsel

DR. BEN CINE VAN A TOTZ
Designer/Illustrator: Joost Swarte
Publisher: De Harmonie/Het Raadsel

JIMBO
Art Director: Art Spiegelman
Illustrator: Gary Panter
Publisher: Pantheon Books

RAW
Art Directors: Art Spiegelman and Francoise Mouly
Illustrator: Joost Swarte
Publisher: Penguin

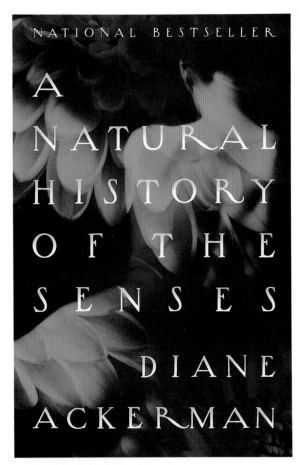

A NATURAL HISTORY OF THE SENSES
Designer: Susan Mitchell
Photographer: Michele Clement
Publisher: Vintage Books

THE PARADISE OF BOMBS
Art Director: Frank Metz
Designer/Illustrator: Fred Marcellino
Publisher: Touchstone

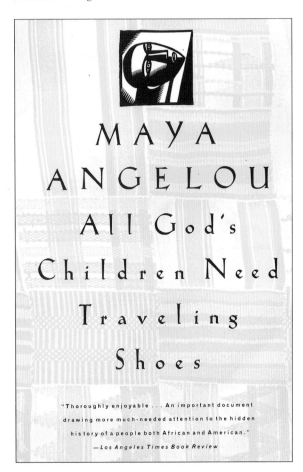

ALL GOD'S CHILDREN NEED TRAVELING SHOES
Art Director: Susan Mitchell   Designer: Adriane Stark
Illustrator: Anthony Russo
Publisher: Vintage Books

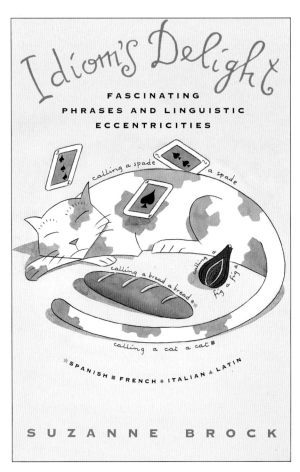

IDIOM'S DELIGHT
Art Director: Susan Mitchell   Designer: Louise Fili
Illustrator: Steven Guarnaccia
Publisher: Vintage Books

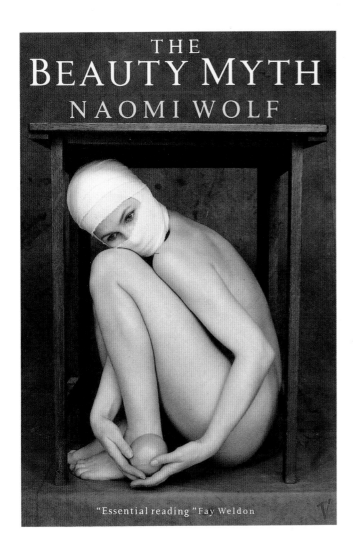

THE BEAUTY MYTH
Designer: Peter Dyer
Photographer: Clare Park/The Special Photographers Company
Publisher: Vintage UK

MADAM I'M ADAM
Designer: Susan Hochbaum
Illustrator: Steven Guarnaccia
Publisher: Scribners

WHY IN THE WORLD
Art Director: Julie Duquet
Designer/Illustrator: Marty Blake
Publisher: Doubleday/Anchor Books

THE BEST FOR LESS
Art Director: Jackie Seow
Designer/Illustrator: Steven Guarnaccia
Publisher: Simon & Shuster

PARIS DREAMBOOK
Art Director: Susan Mitchell   Designer: Adriane Stark
Photographers: Issaku Fujita/Photonica; The Douglas Brothers
Publisher: Vintage Books

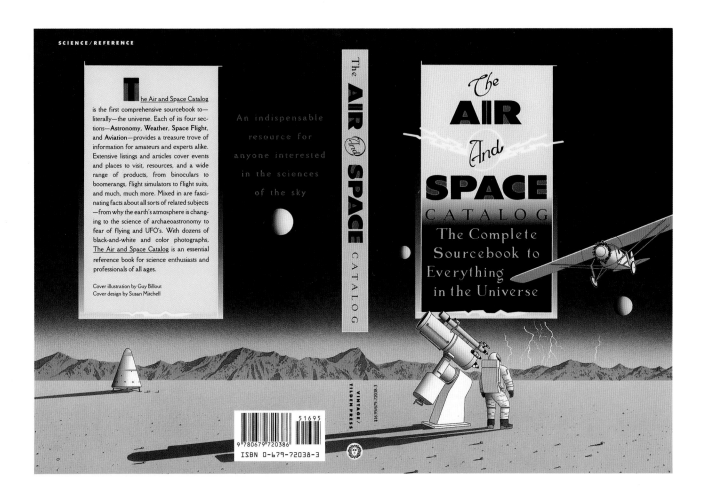

SCIENCE/REFERENCE

The Air and Space Catalog
is the first comprehensive sourcebook to—
literally—the universe. Each of its four sec-
tions—**Astronomy**, **Weather**, **Space Flight**,
and **Aviation**—provides a treasure trove of
information for amateurs and experts alike.
Extensive listings and articles cover events
and places to visit, resources, and a wide
range of products, from binoculars to
boomerangs, flight simulators to flight suits,
and much, much more. Mixed in are fascinating facts about all sorts of related subjects
—from why the earth's atmosphere is changing to the science of archaeoastronomy to
fear of flying and UFO's. With dozens of
black-and-white and color photographs,
The Air and Space Catalog is an essential
reference book for science enthusiasts and
professionals of all ages.

Cover illustration by Guy Billout
Cover design by Susan Mitchell

An indispensable
resource for
anyone interested
in the sciences
of the sky

The
AIR
And
SPACE
CATALOG

The
AIR
And
SPACE
CATALOG
The Complete
Sourcebook to
Everything
in the Universe

VINTAGE/
TILDEN PRESS

ISBN 0-679-72038-3

THE AIR AND SPACE CATALOG
Art Director/Designer: Susan Mitchell
Illustrator: Guy Billout
Publisher: Vintage Books

ON FLOWERS

Designer: Michael Mabry
Photographer: Kathryn Kleinman
Publisher: Chronicle Books

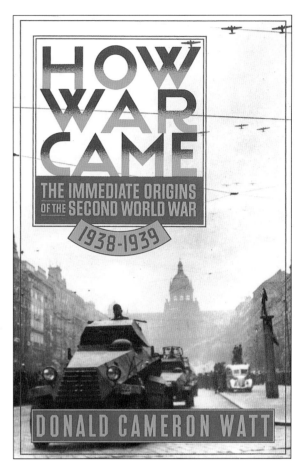

LUTHER
Art Director: Kathy Kikkert
Designer: Joe Cuticone
Publisher: Doubleday

HOW WAR CAME
Art Director: Louise Fili   Designer: Jon Valk
Photographer: Popper Photo
Publisher: Pantheon Books

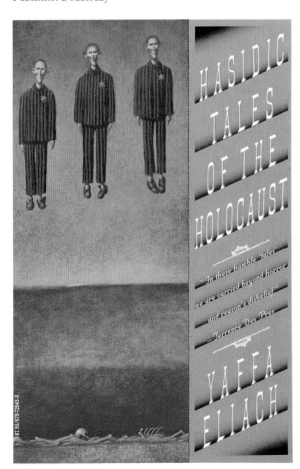

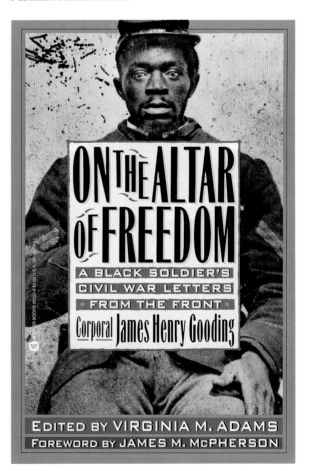

HASIDIC TALES OF THE HOLOCAUST
Art Director/Designer: Susan Mitchell
Illustrator: Tom Curry
Publisher: Vintage Books

ON THE ALTAR OF FREEDOM
Art Director: Jackie Merri Meyer   Designer: Tom McKeveny
Photography: Bettmann Archive
Publisher: Warner Books

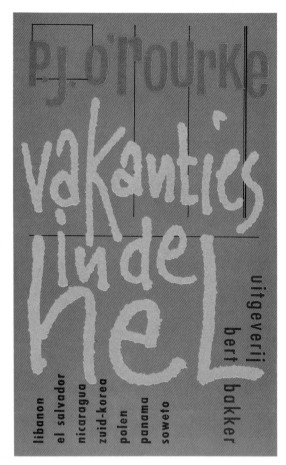

VAKANTIES IN DE HEL
Designer: Rick Vermeulen, Hard Werken Design
Publisher: Uitgeverij Bert Bakker

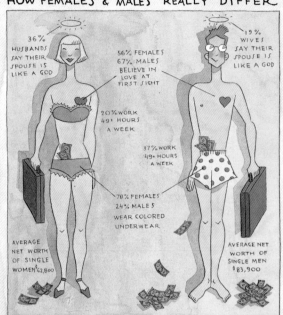

THE GREAT DIVIDE
Designer/Illustrator: Steven Guarnaccia
Publisher: Poseidon Press

I'M SO HAPPY
Designer: Jo Bonney   Art Director: Susan Mitchell
Illustrator: Jeanne Fisher   Photographer: Dennis Hallinan
Publisher: Vintage Books

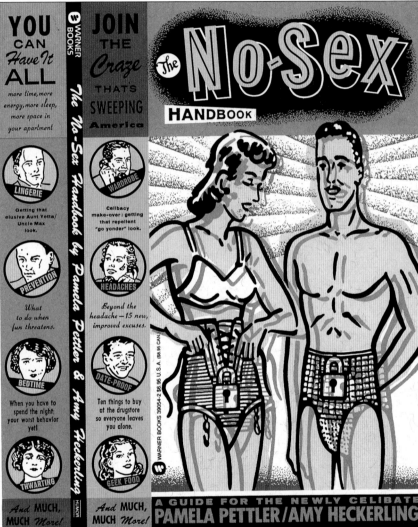

THE NO-SEX HANDBOOK
Art Director: Jackie Merri Meyer
Designer: Charles S. Anderson
Publisher: Warner Books

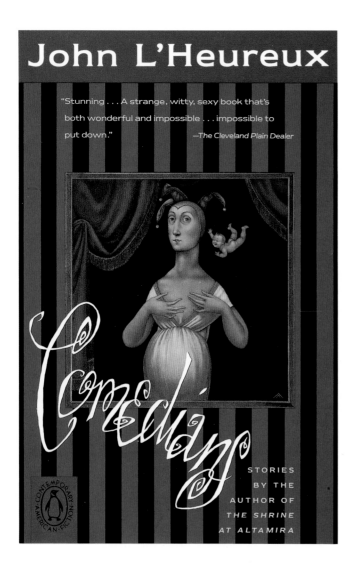

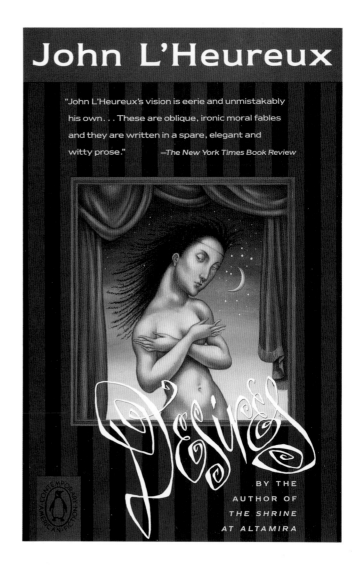

AMERICAN CONTEMPORARY FICTION
Art Director/Designer: Michael Ian Kaye
Illustrator: Anita Kunz   Typographer: Robert Clyde Anderson
Publisher: Viking Penguin

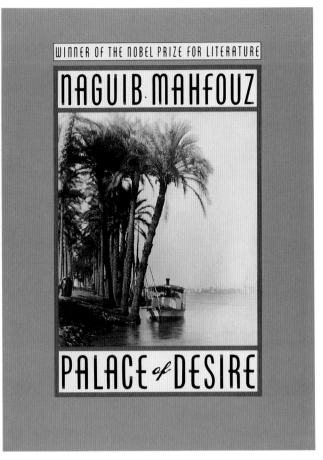

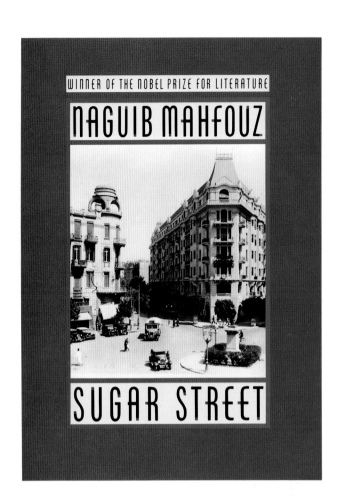

CAIRO TRILOGY
Art Directors: Alex Gotfryd and Peter Kruzan
Designer: Carin Golberg Photography: Culver Pictures
Publisher: Doubleday

VINTAGE CLASSICS
Art Director/Designer: Susan Mitchell
Illustrator: Sally Mara Sturman
Publisher: Vintage Books

BERTOLD BRECHT SERIES
Art Director: Krystyna Skalski
Designer: Jo Bonney   Illustrator: John Howard
Publisher: Grove Weidenfeld

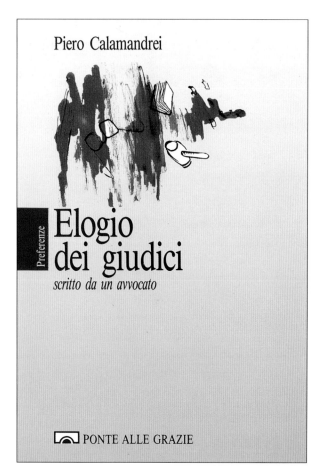

Piero Calamandrei

Elogio dei giudici
scritto da un avvocato

PONTE ALLE GRAZIE

Jacques Ruffié

Il sesso e la morte
Prefazione di Giorgio Celli

IL PONTE EDITORI

PREFERENZE
Designer: Andrea Rauch, Graphiti
Illustrator: *(left)* Gianpaolo Di Cocco
Publisher: Ponte Alle Grazie

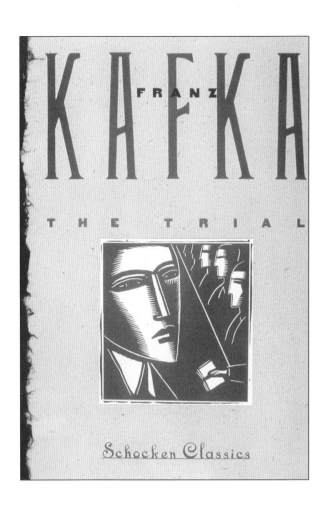

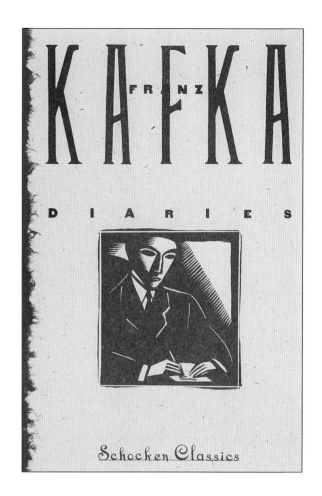

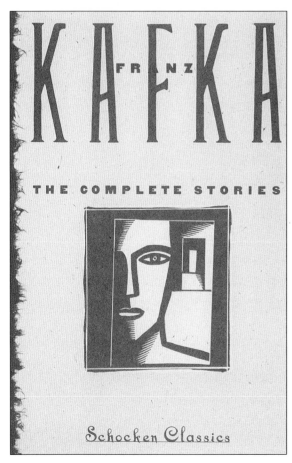

KAFKA SERIES
Art Director/Designer: Louise Fili
Illustrator: Anthony Russo
Publisher: Pantheon/Schocken

One, No One & One Hundred Thousand

TRANSLATED BY

Luigi Pirandello

WILLIAM WEAVER

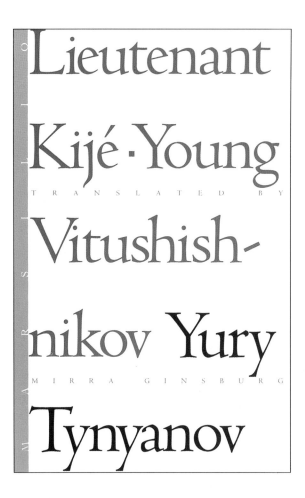

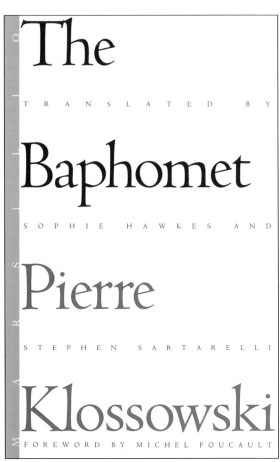

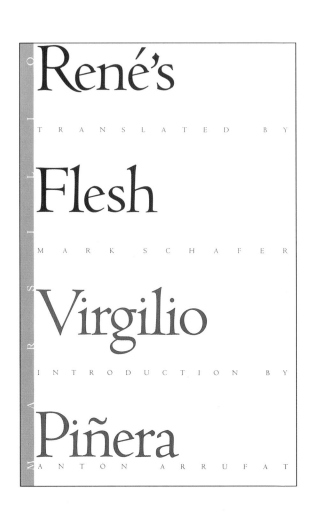

MARSILIO FICTION SERIES
Art Director/Designer: Louise Fili
Publisher: Marsilio

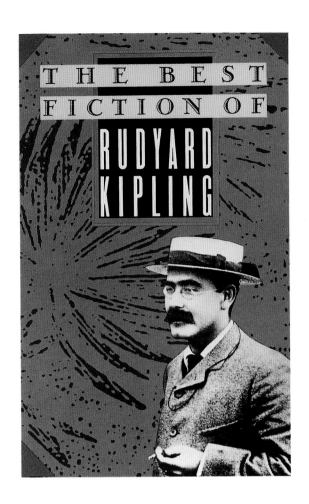

KIPLING SERIES
Art Director: Alex Gotfryd
Designer: Carin Goldberg
Publisher: Doubleday/Anchor Books

THE GUARDIAN BOOK SERIES
Art Director/Designer: Senate Design Ltd.
Illustrator: *(left)* Ian Anderson   Cartoonist: *(right)* David Austin
Publisher: Fourth Estate

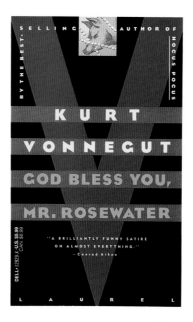

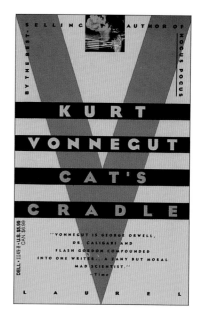

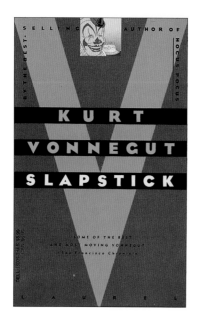

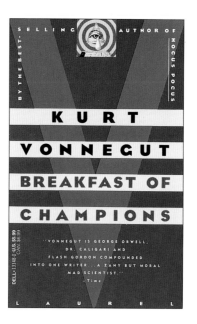

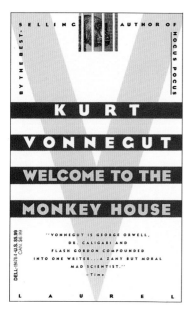

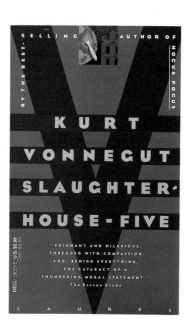

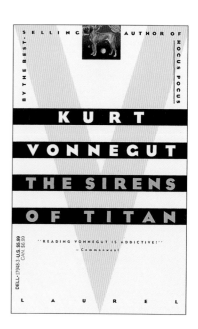

KURT VONNEGUT SERIES
Art Director: Gerald Counihan
Designer: Carin Goldberg
Publisher: Dell Publishing

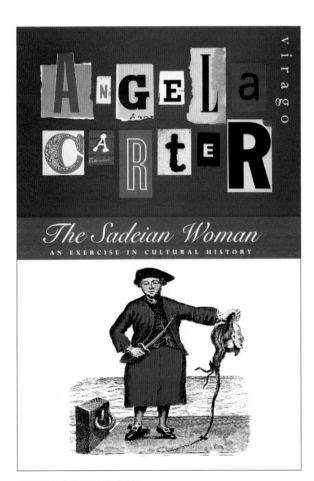

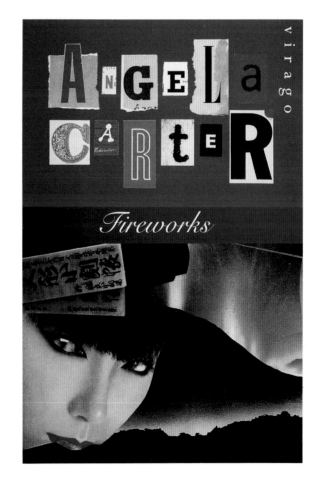

ANGELA CARTER SERIES
Designer: Senate Design Ltd.
Illustrators: *(top left, bottom right)* Irene von Treskow, *(top right)* Alex Carter, *(bottom left)* The Mansell Collection Limited
Publisher: Virago

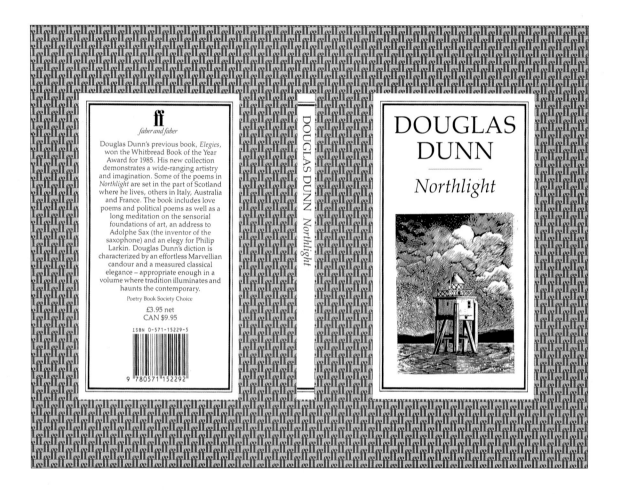

DOUGLAS DUNN

Northlight

DOUGLAS DUNN *Northlight*

ff

faber and faber

Douglas Dunn's previous book, *Elegies*, won the Whitbread Book of the Year Award for 1985. His new collection demonstrates a wide-ranging artistry and imagination. Some of the poems in *Northlight* are set in the part of Scotland where he lives, others in Italy, Australia and France. The book includes love poems and political poems as well as a long meditation on the sensorial foundations of art, an address to Adolphe Sax (the inventor of the saxophone) and an elegy for Philip Larkin. Douglas Dunn's diction is characterized by an effortless Marvellian candour and a measured classical elegance – appropriate enough in a volume where tradition illuminates and haunts the contemporary.

Poetry Book Society Choice

£3.95 net
CAN $9.95

ISBN 0-571-15229-5

9 780571 152292

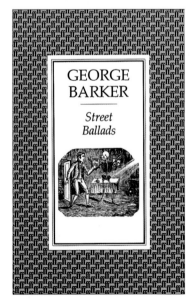

GEORGE
BARKER

*Street
Ballads*

PHILIP
GROSS

*The Son of the
Duke of Nowhere*

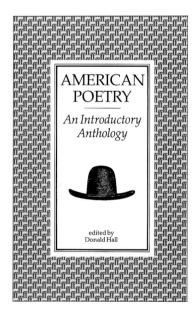

AMERICAN
POETRY

*An Introductory
Anthology*

edited by
Donald Hall

POETRY SERIES
Art Director: John McConnell, Pentagram
Designer: Jason Godfrey
Publisher: Faber and Faber

108

RANDOM HOUSE KEYNOTES

OF MICE AND MEN
JOHN STEINBECK

A BOLD NEW APPROACH
TO STUDY GUIDES

A RAPID REVIEW OF:
· PLOT SUMMARY
· CHARACTER SKETCHES
· MAIN THEMES & IDEAS
· STYLE & STRUCTURE
· SYMBOLISM
· CRITICAL ANALYSIS

RANDOM HOUSE KEYNOTES

THE JUNGLE
UPTON SINCLAIR

A BOLD NEW APPROACH
TO STUDY GUIDES

A RAPID REVIEW OF:
· PLOT SUMMARY
· CHARACTER SKETCHES
· MAIN THEMES & IDEAS
· STYLE & STRUCTURE
· SYMBOLISM
· CRITICAL ANALYSIS

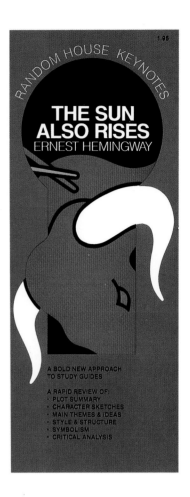

RANDOM HOUSE KEYNOTES

THE SUN ALSO RISES
ERNEST HEMINGWAY

A BOLD NEW APPROACH
TO STUDY GUIDES

A RAPID REVIEW OF:
· PLOT SUMMARY
· CHARACTER SKETCHES
· MAIN THEMES & IDEAS
· STYLE & STRUCTURE
· SYMBOLISM
· CRITICAL ANALYSIS

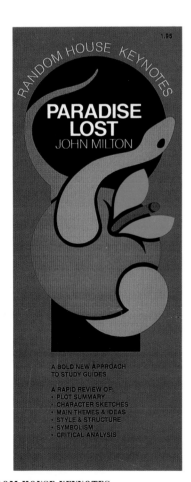

RANDOM HOUSE KEYNOTES

PARADISE LOST
JOHN MILTON

A BOLD NEW APPROACH
TO STUDY GUIDES

A RAPID REVIEW OF:
· PLOT SUMMARY
· CHARACTER SKETCHES
· MAIN THEMES & IDEAS
· STYLE & STRUCTURE
· SYMBOLISM
· CRITICAL ANALYSIS

RANDOM HOUSE KEYNOTES

MOBY-DICK
HERMAN MELVILLE

A BOLD NEW APPROACH
TO STUDY GUIDES

A RAPID REVIEW OF:
· PLOT SUMMARY
· CHARACTER SKETCHES
· MAIN THEMES & IDEAS
· STYLE & STRUCTURE
· SYMBOLISM
· CRITICAL ANALYSIS

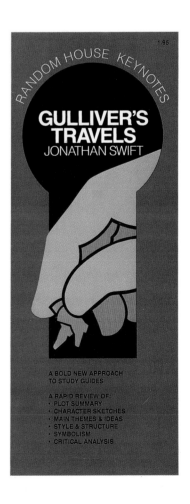

RANDOM HOUSE KEYNOTES

GULLIVER'S TRAVELS
JONATHAN SWIFT

A BOLD NEW APPROACH
TO STUDY GUIDES

A RAPID REVIEW OF:
· PLOT SUMMARY
· CHARACTER SKETCHES
· MAIN THEMES & IDEAS
· STYLE & STRUCTURE
· SYMBOLISM
· CRITICAL ANALYSIS

RANDOM HOUSE KEYNOTES
Art Director: Robert Scudellari
Designer/Illustrator: Peter Bradford
Publisher: Random House

Series

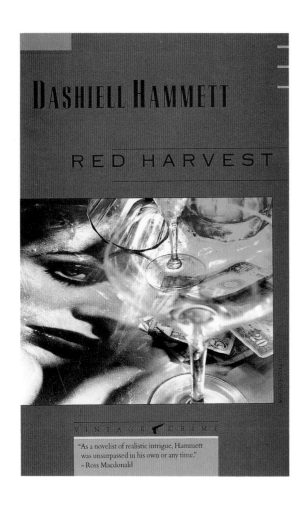

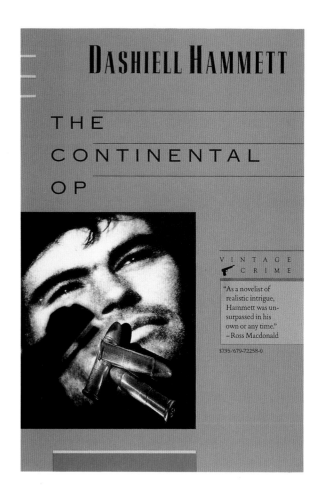

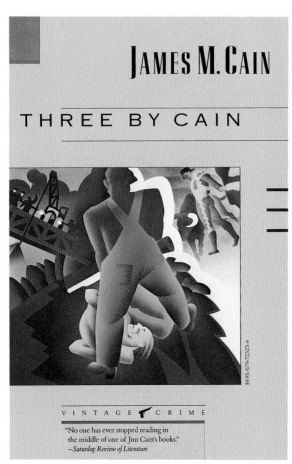

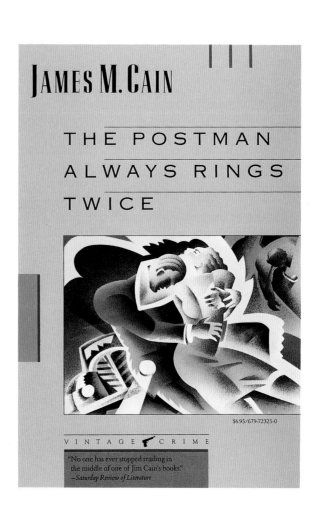

VINTAGE CRIME
Art Director: Susan Mitchell Designer: Keith Sheridan Associates, Inc.
Illustrator: (*bottom*) James Steinberg Photographer: (*top*) Axel Crieger
Publisher: Vintage Books

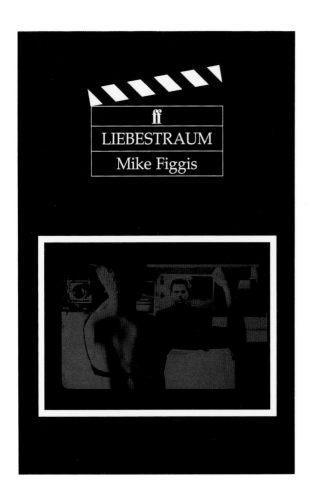

ff

LIEBESTRAUM

Mike Figgis

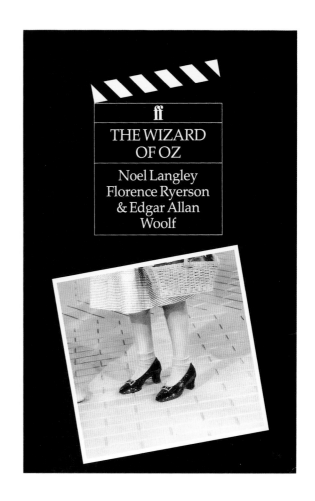

ff

THE WIZARD
OF OZ

Noel Langley
Florence Ryerson
& Edgar Allan
Woolf

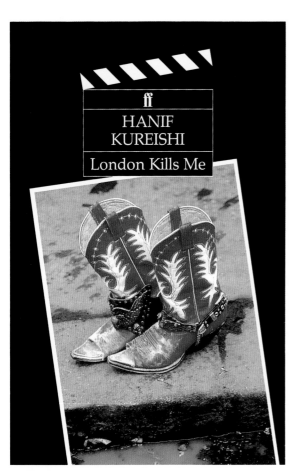

ff

HANIF
KUREISHI

London Kills Me

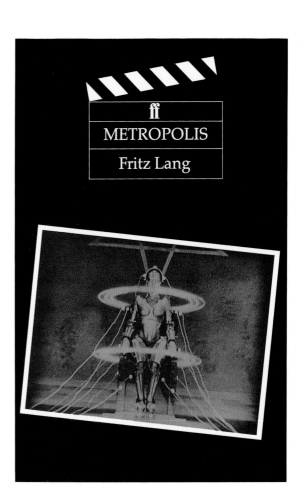

ff

METROPOLIS

Fritz Lang

FILM SERIES
Art Director: John McConnell, Pentagram   Designer: Jason Godfrey
Photographers: *(top left)* United International Pictures, *(top right)* Metro-Goldwyn-Mayer,
(bottom left) Jacques Prayer/Gamma   Publisher: Faber and Faber

THE BURGLAR

"If Jack Kerouac had written crime novels, they might have sounded a bit like this."
—Geoffrey O'Brien

Nat Harbin is a family man. His family happens to be a gang of burglars. Now Nat has met a woman so hypnotically seductive that he will leave his partners and his trade to possess her. But you don't get away from family that easily.

The Burglar has the hallmarks that made David Goodis one of the great practitioners of the hard-boiled crime novel: a haunting identification with life's losers, and a hero who finds out who he is only by betraying everything he believes in.

Cover design by Keith Sheridan Associates, Inc.
Cover photography by Alesia Exum

FICTION/CRIME

VINTAGE CRIME

$8.00
$10.95

ISBN 0-679-73472-4

9 780679 734727 50800>

david GOODIS

the BURGLAR

A dreamlike masterpiece of crime, honor, and perverse loyalty by the legendary author of *Shoot the Piano Player*

VINTAGE CRIME

THE FAR CRY

Once upon a time, in a lonely house near Taos, a girl named Jenny Ames was murdered. No one knew where she had come from, or why she had died, or what had become of her killer. Eight years later a troubled man named George Weaver moved into the same house and discovered that nothing is more treacherously seductive than an unsolved murder. Unless it's a beautiful and enigmatic victim.

The Far Cry is at once a seamlessly constructed novel of detection and a harrowing portrayal of psychic meltdown by a legendary practitioner of the art of suspense.

Cover design by Keith Sheridan Associates, Inc.
Cover photography by Uwe Blum

FICTION/CRIME

VINTAGE CRIME

U.S. $8.00
CAN. $10.95

ISBN 0-679-73469-4

9 780679 734697 50800>

fredric BROWN

the FAR CRY

"Fredric Brown is my favorite writer of all time."
—Mickey Spillane

the FAR CRY

fredric BROWN

VINTAGE CRIME

VINTAGE CRIME BLACK LIZARD
Art Director: Susan Mitchell
Designer: Keith Sheridan Associates, Inc.   Photographers: *(top)* Alesia Exum, *(bottom)* Uwe Blum
Publisher: Vintage Books

 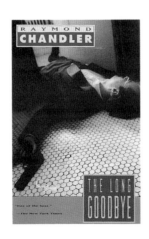  

VINTAGE CRIME BLACK LIZARD
Art Director: Susan Mitchell   Designer: Keith Sheridan Associates, Inc.
Photographers: Gary Isaacs all except *The Lady in the Lake*, Barnaby Hall
Publisher: Vintage Books

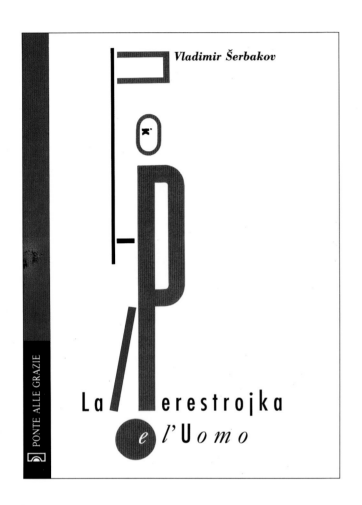

Vladimir Šerbakov

La Perestrojka e l'Uomo

PONTE ALLE GRAZIE

Ruslan Khasbulatov

SOCIALISMO e Burocrazia

PONTE ALLE GRAZIE

FIAMMELLE
Designer: Stefano Rovai, Graphiti
Publisher: Ponte Alle Grazie

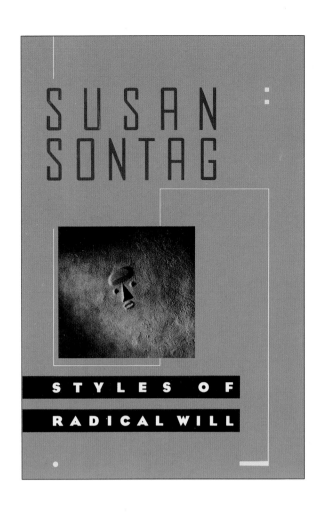

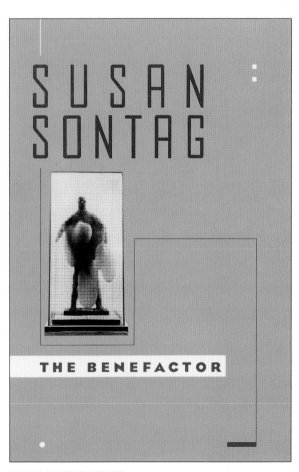

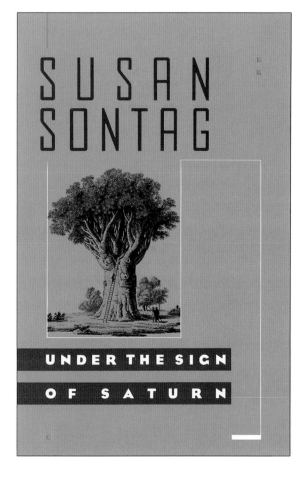

SUSAN SONTAG SERIES
Art Director: Julie Duquet   Designer: Carin Goldberg
Artists: *(top left)* Isamu Noguchi, *(bottom left)* Garnett Puett, *(bottom right)* Alexander von Humboldt and Aime Bonplaud from
Atlas pittoresques...1810   Photographer: *(top right)* Virginia Cuthbert Elliott Collection   Publisher: Anchor Books

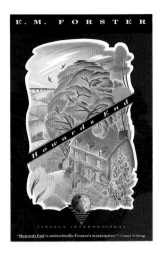

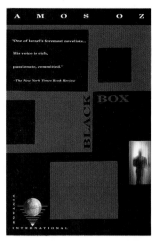

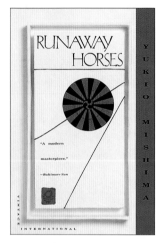

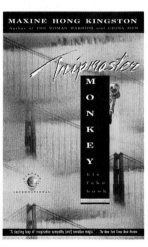

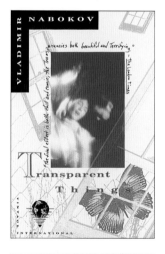

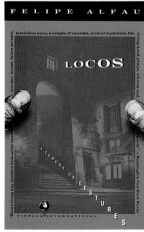

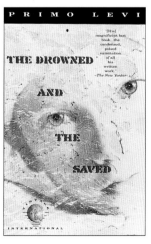

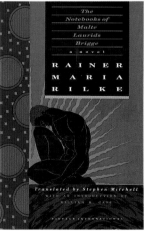

VINTAGE INTERNATIONAL

Art Director: Susan Mitchell   Designer: Marc Cohen   Illustrators: *Howard's*...Jenny Tylden-Wright   *The Fifth*...
Andrezej Dudzinski   *Barrabas* Benno Friedman   *Transparent*...and *(opposite) Look*...Barnaby Hall   *The Drowned*...Therese Kopin
The Notebooks...John Martinez   *Ulysses* Angela Armet   Artist: *G. A Novel* Caravaggio   Photographers: *Black Box*...Arthur Tress
About Looking Gary Winogrand   *Tripmaster*...Barnaby Hall and Ken Skalski   *Exile*...Paul Rackley   Publisher: Vintage Books

116

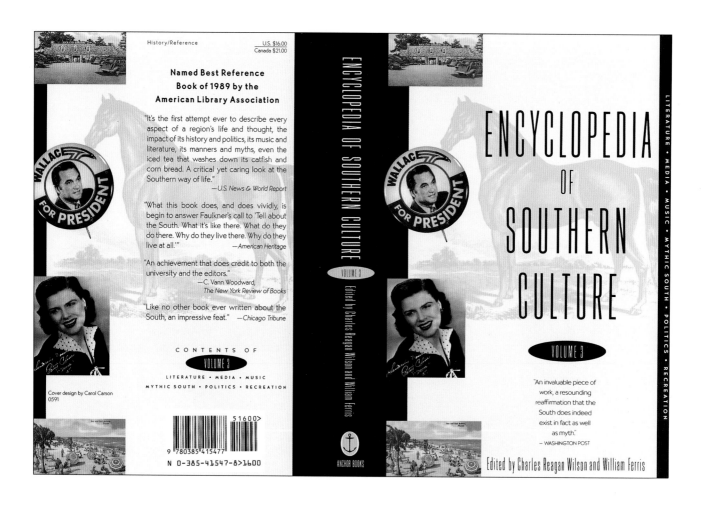

ENCYCLOPEDIA OF SOUTHERN CULTURE
Art Director: Julie Duquet
Designer: Carol Carson
Publisher: Doubleday/Anchor Books

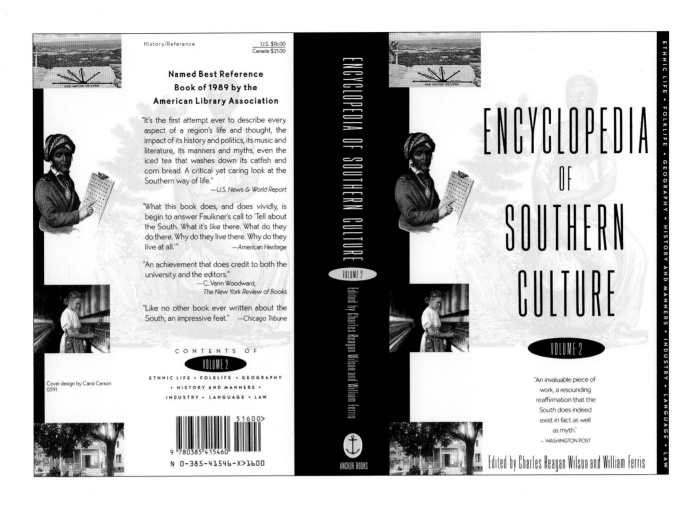

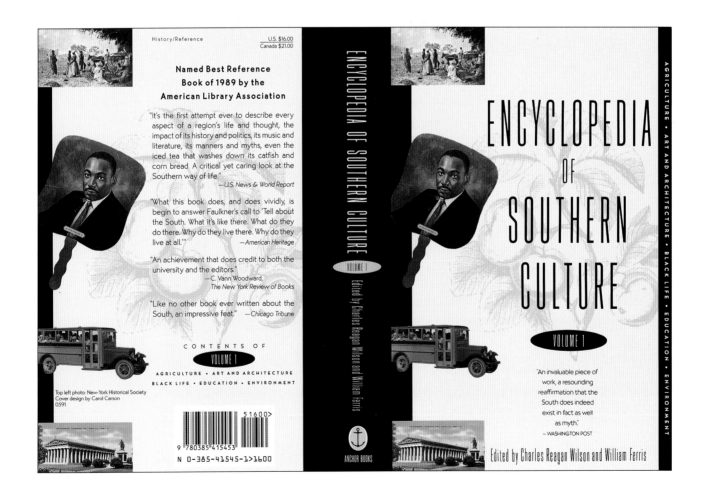

The text visible within the first image (Soho Square III cover):

Soho Square III Editor Alberto Manguel

Mary Maher – Irish Times

Angela Carter
Sharon Thesen
Albert Wendt
Jenny Bornholdt
Vincent O'Sullivan
Philip Davison
Glyn Maxwell
Margaret Mahy
Dinah Hawken
Salman Rushdie
Robert Crawford
Jane Campion
Seamus Heaney
Lloyd Jones
Padgett Powell
Simeon Dumdum Jr
Owen Marshall
Philip Salom

Damien Wilkins
Elizabeth Knox
Jorie Graham
Elizabeth Jolley
Charles Causley
Hone Tuwhare
Helen Garner
Elizabeth Smither
Barbara Anderson
Bernadette Hall
Joan London
Lauren Holder
Michael Ondaatje
Ian Wedde
Eavan Boland
Michael Carson
Gregory O'Brien
Gerald Murnane
John Ashbery

For the third year running, Bloomsbury has produced a Christmas pudding for the discerning reader of eclectic tastes, a richly varied mixture of unpredictable bits from places far and near. The annual miscellany has established itself on surprise value; apart from a deliberate policy of including lesser-known writers with famous names, the selection of material is entirely in the editor's gift..... All in all, an exotic sampler that could prove a crisp antidote to the excessive Victoriana of the season..

SOHO SQUARE

ISBN 0-7475-1022-9

9 780747 510222

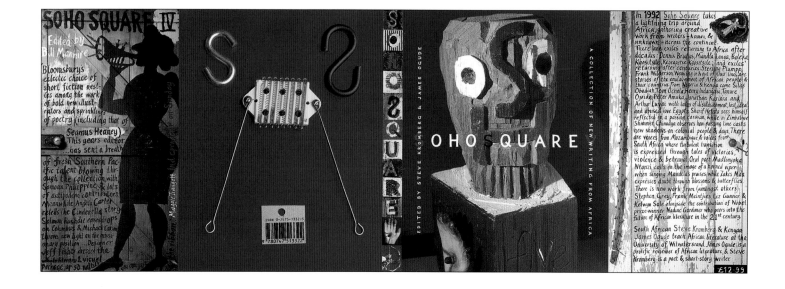

The text visible within the second image (Soho Square IV cover):

SOHO SQUARE IV

Edited by Bill Manhire

Bloomsbury's eclectic choice of short fiction nestles among the work of bold new illustrators and sprinklings of poetry (including that of Seamus Heaney). This year's editor ...has sent a breath of fresh Southern Pacific talent blowing through the collection with Samoan Philip Prince & lots of antipodean contributors. Meanwhile Angela Carter retells the Cinderella story. Salman Rushdie eavesdrops on Columbus & Michael Carson throws new light on the missionary position. Designer Jeff Fisher dressed the whole literary & visual package up so nattily.

ISBN 0-7475-1332-5

9 780747 513322

OHO SQUARE

In 1992 Soho Square takes a lightning trip around Africa, gathering creative work from writers – known & unknown – across the continent. There are exiles returning to Africa after decades: Dennis Brutus, Mandla Langa, Baleka Kgositsile, Keorapetse Kgositsile; and exiles returning after centuries Sterling Plumpp, Frank Wilderson. Weaving in & out of these lines are stories of the enslavement of African people & their countries. From Nigeria & Kenya come Silas Obadiah, Tom Ochola, Henry Indangasi, Tanure Ojaide, Peter Amuka, Jonathan Kariara and Arthur Luvai with tales of disillusionment, lost ideals and abused love. Egypt's Sherif Hetata sees himself reflected in a passing caravan while in Zimbabwe Shimmer Chinodya observes how passing time casts new shadows on colonial people & days. There are voices from Mozambique & voices from South Africa where turbulent transition is expressed through tales of victories, violence & betrayal. Oral poet Madlinyoka Ntanzi calls on the image of a horned viper when singing Mandela's praises while Zakes Mda expresses doubt through blossoms & butterflies. There is new work from (amongst others) Stephen Gray, Frank Meintjies, Liz Gunner & Kelwyn Sole alongside the contribution of Nobel prize-winner Nadine Gordimer who peers into the future of African literature in the 21st century.

South African Steve Kromberg & Kenyan James Ogude teach African literature at the University of Witwatersrand. James Ogude is a prolific reviewer of African literature & Steve Kromberg is a poet & short-story writer.

A COLLECTION OF NEW WRITING FROM AFRICA

EDITED BY STEVE KROMBERG & JAMES OGUDE

£12.99

SOHO SQUARE
Designer/Illustrator: Jeffrey Fisher
Publisher: Bloomsbury Press

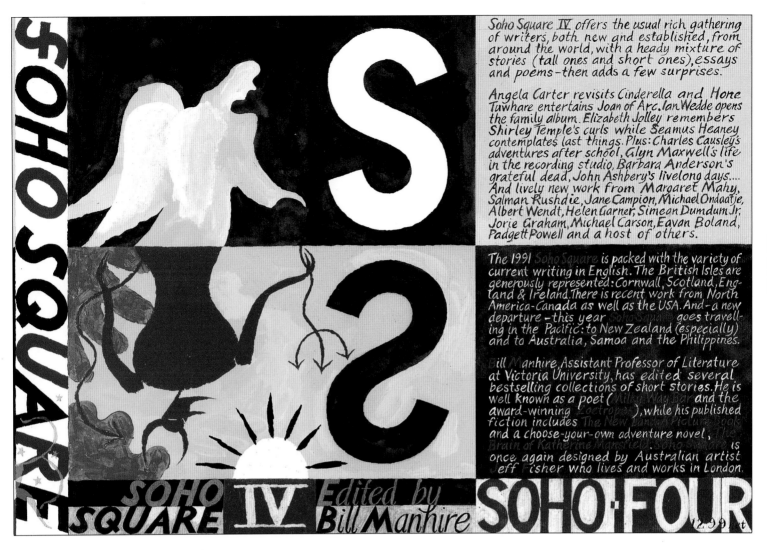

ES SERIES
Artist: *(left)* Filippo Lippi, 1440, *(right)* Eugene de Blass, 1911
Publisher: ES

SE SERIES

Artist: *(top left)* J.J. Audubon, 1835, *(top right)* René Magritte,
(bottom left) Salvador Dali, 1904 , *(bottom right)* Hiroshige
Publisher: Studio Editoriale

BY THE EARLY 1900S MAGAZINES WERE THE PRIMARY NEWS AND ENTERTAINMENT MEDIUM IN THE INDUSTRIAL WORLD. REPORTEDLY OVER ONE HUNDRED THOUSAND DIFFERENT TITLES WERE PUBLISHED IN THE UNITED STATES ALONE. THESE INCLUDED MAGAZINES ON VIRTUALLY EVERY POPULAR AND ARCANE SUBJECT FROM AGRICULTURE TO ZOOLOGY, WITH THE MOST UBIQUITOUS— FASHION, HOUSEHOLD, AND NEWS MAGAZINES—AGGRESSIVELY VYING FOR ATTENTION IN AN EVER-EXPANDING MARKETPLACE. THIS PERIOD MARKED THE BIRTH OF A MASS MARKET. ADVANCED TECHNOLOGY ALLOWED LARGE PRINT RUNS. IMPROVED TRANSPORTATION OFFERED WIDE DISTRIBUTION. AND INCREASED LITERACY FOSTERED A WORLDWIDE DEMAND FOR THESE EPHEMERAL STOREHOUSES OF FACT AND FICTION. SOME SAY MAGAZINES WERE NEVER AS GOOD AS DURING THE YEARS BETWEEN THE FIN DE SIECLE AND THE MID-1930S. MANY IMPORTANT MAGAZINES WERE BORN AND FLOURISHED DURING THIS CRITICAL TIME, LONG BEFORE TELE-VISION USURPED BOTH ADVERTISING AND AUDIENCE.

IT WAS A GOLDEN AGE IN MANY WAYS, PARTICULARLY FOR THE MASS CIRCULATION MAGAZINES. FROM THE MARKETING PERSPECTIVE THE COMPETITION WAS STIFF—CIRCULATION WARS WERE COMMON—BUT SINCE THE PRINT MEDIA ENJOYED A VIRTUAL COMMUNICATIONS MONOPOLY, SELLING THE PRODUCT WAS NOT AS COMPLEX AS IT IS TODAY. THE MOST POPULAR MAGAZINES GARNERED CIRCULATIONS IN THE MILLIONS— HENRY LUCE'S *LIFE*, FOR EXAMPLE, WAS A FIXTURE IN MOST AMERICAN HOUSEHOLDS—BUT EVEN LESS POPU-LAR MAGAZINES WERE SUPPORTED BY A CONSIDERABLY SMALLER NUMBER OF READERS. WHILE EVERY MAGA-ZINE FOUGHT FOR THE SCOOP THAT WOULD INCREASE THEIR READERSHIP, IF ONLY FOR THE MOMENT, THE FACT that readers invariably turned to magazines for a variety of basic needs offered benefits to the publishers and their staffs that are today unheard of in the brutally competitive marketplace. One significant difference between then and now was how covers were designed.

Unique to this golden age was the fact that a great many magazine covers were tabula rasa; not locked into inflexible formats but rather so mutable that often they totally changed—from the masthead to the image—with virtually every issue. The original *Life* (the American humor magazine), *Vanity Fair, Asia, The Delineator, Charm*, and *Vogue* are just a few of the many periodicals whose superbly designed, often quite imaginative covers were rarely ever the same from month to month. Others, including *Fortune* and *The Saturday Evening Post,* maintained a consistent masthead (or logo) but allowed distinctive artwork to drive their editorial personalities. More important, coverlines were restrained and sometimes eliminated entirely to preserve the integrity of a striking piece of art. Today, almost seventy years after its founding, the venerable *New Yorker* is the only publication among the mass market newsstand magazines to continue this currently anachronistic practice of eliminating coverlines (although recently they have been printed on a separate flap).

In the current market the magazine cover is an invaluable piece of editorial real estate. Fred Woodward, art director of *Rolling Stone*, admits that even after two decades of profitable publishing, which suggests a solid readership, certain issues of his magazine still sell better than others owing entirely to the cover image. Who the cover celebrity is—how popular he or she is at that time—is a major selling point. For example, in 1992 Madonna was the most commercial cover girl in the United States, and therefore it was no surprise that she appeared on three magazines simultaneously —including *Newsweek*—and on at least a dozen others during the same year. Similarly, each year like clockwork *Sports Illustrated's* circulation enjoys a sharp increase with the famous swimsuit issue. Although it does not rely on a celebrity, it nevertheless exploits another prime selling tool, sex. It goes without saying that a striking cover will attract more readers than a mundane one, and a sexy cover offers even greater benefits. Yet the majority of newsstand magazines have no logical reason to publish a Madonna or swimsuit photograph; hence, most magazines rely on coverlines to whet the reader's appetites with their tastiest ingredients. At the same time, however, the designer's ability to produce a truly powerful cover image is dampened by a flood of excesses.

If one were to describe the single worst pox on magazine cover design among the numerous taboos and rules laid down by publishers and marketing experts, the overuse of coverlines is it. While some coverline treatments are handled well *(Rolling Stone's* are typically elegant, and *Interview's* are often fashionably raucous), most are applied without intelligence, and they are usually squeezed and contorted onto the image area with all manner of anamorphic distortion. Coverlines are consistently viewed by designers as roadblocks along what for many has become a designer's no-man's land. In fact, out of frustration some designers simply devote all their energies to the magazine's insides which are comparatively unhampered.

Nevertheless coverlines serve a function, to provide a billboard of contents that is necessary for making an impulse purchase. Since most newsstand magazines are aimed at people on the go—at airports, train and bus stations, and on supermarket lines—if a cover image is not arresting—which is frequently the case—coverlines slow the reader down just long enough to impart important information about their potential purchase. In a competitive market coverlines, particularly those signaling content different from that conveyed through the cover image, potentially can increase sales. A problem develops when the needs of the editor and marketer—to inform and promote—clash with those of the designer and art director—to organize and aestheticize. Cluttering up a cover with too much type, frequently in various weights and styles, often hamstrings designers from doing their best work. Since coverlines are inherently problematic, making the most of them is often the litmus test of the good magazine designer. If they are accessible and handsome, then the designer has successfully solved the problem. If they are obtrusive and jumbled, then the design should be seen as a failure. Unfortunately, however, success and failure are relative: a successful magazine cover is not necessarily a well-designed one. Similarly, beautifully designed covers may not be great sellers.

Such is the nature of the business as reflected by public taste. While these tastes are varied, for the most part the public is oblivious to the fine points of graphic design. The general public might not shun a beautifully designed cover, but judging from the evidence in the marketplace, rarely will they boycott a poorly designed one either. Regardless of its cover, as long as the magazine fulfills its basic mission the consumer is content. Therefore it is the job of the art director and designer, in concert with the editor, to create covers that transcend common convention and basic need. As suggested by the paucity in this book of exemplary mass market magazine covers in the areas of news, general interest, travel, fashion, and lifestyle this is a daunting task. The common demand that a cover conform to certain stifling "industry standards" invariably produces negative results. When the celebrated English designer Neville Brody was asked to submit what he considered were his best covers to this book he replied that covers were the weakest part of his overall magazine design. One might argue that his covers for the fashion/culture magazines *The Face* and *Arena* were well executed—indeed well suited to the content and readership of the respective magazines—but one must also agree that they were not as exciting as the interior design, nor others as unconventional as more avant-garde publications featuring similar content.

Given the various constraints how does one determine what is "great" magazine cover design? Contemporary covers should not be judged against the past because the best covers of the golden age were produced in a completely different commercial and cultural milieu which is inapplicable today (although many of those covers should be respected as paradigms of a certain era of design and illustration). Nor should they be judged against today's standards because contemporary methods for selling magazines are often rooted in pseudo-science, such as focus groups, which has little appreciation for the aesthetics of good design. So can they be judged against each other? While this is a better touchstone it is still flawed since magazines are aimed at scores of different consumers and each must be responsive to their audience's preferences. A successful cover must be imaginative while definitely appealing to its audience. Therefore, an exemplary news magazine cover should not be compared to an exemplary fashion or art magazine cover where different criteria apply. A mass market fashion magazine cover cannot be compared to an avant-garde one, either, but must be judged on its own particular merits. Even magazines within a single genre, such as newspaper magazine supplements, are often rooted in different criteria, such as will it be sold separately from its host publication or not. Perhaps the best way to determine what is best is by what is effective given the marketplace itself. If a cover is imaginatively conceived given the constraints of its genre, then it is a great cover.

Of course, the term "great" is imprecise. Marketing experts will indeed argue that what designers consider great is beyond the ken of the average consumer, while designers will counter that what is great for marketing experts ignores aesthetics that challenge convention. This book errs in favor of the designer's criteria. The covers selected here are not necessarily commercial successes—indeed that question was not even broached—but they do represent the most ambitious (or challenging) use of materials and resources within their particular genres. Yet the use of cutting edge or fashionable design conceits and styles is not a ticket for inclusion. Great magazine covers are not the ones that blindly follow the dominant trends no matter how well done they are. Rather the magazine covers that truly deserve the kudos are ones that meet any of the following standards: Challenge the status quo, whatever the convention may be; exhibit a distinct personality through type and/or image; or make the most out of limitations.

In the harsh light of current magazine publishing the covers selected here may reveal some blemishes—few are flawless—but they also exhibit an art director and designer's vision. And it is that quality that separates the innovative from the formulaic and the original from the follower.

CAPE

CAPE
Designers: Peter Dyer and Conor Brady
Photographer: Thomas Wattenberg/dpa
Publisher: Jonathan Cape

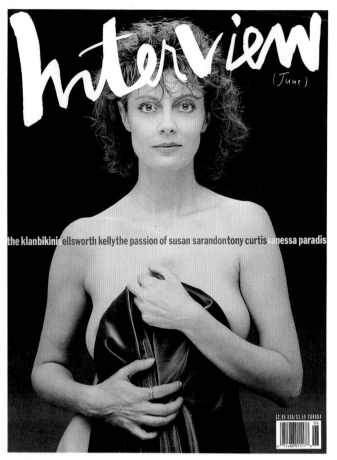

INTERVIEW
Creative Director: Tibor Kalman   Designer: Richard Pandisco
Photographer: The Estate of Robert Mapplethorpe
Publisher: Brant Publications, Inc.

INTERVIEW
Creative Director: Fabien Baron
Photographer: Wayne Maser
Publisher: Brant Publications, Inc.

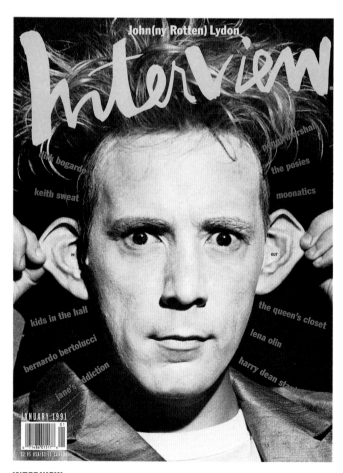

INTERVIEW
Creative Director: Tibor Kalman
Photographer: Kurt Markus
Publisher: Brant Publications, Inc.

INTERVIEW
Creative Director: Fabien Baron
Photographer: Herb Ritts
Publisher: Brant Publications, Inc.

SONOMA STYLE
Art Director/Illustrator: Kathleen Nelson
Publisher: Sonoma Style Magazine Inc.

BEACH CULTURE
Art Director/Designer: David Carson
Photographer: Matt Mahurin
Publisher: Surfer Publications Inc.

PREMIERE
Art Director: Xavier Boure
Photography: Collection of Christophe L. Drapeau
Publisher: SEDPP

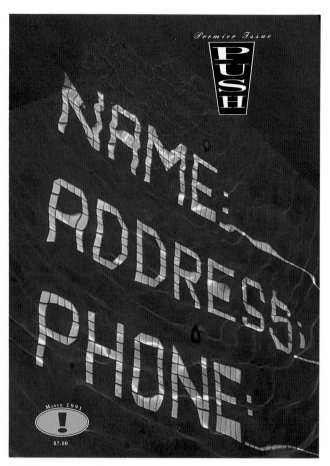

PUSH
Art Director: Lloyd Ziff
Designers: Lloyd Ziff and Giovanni Russo   Photographer: Edward Ruscha
Publisher: Push! Communications, Inc.

LIRE
Designers: Walter Bernard and Milton Glaser, WBMG, Inc.
Illustrator: Mirko Ilic
Publisher: Groupe Express & Compagnie

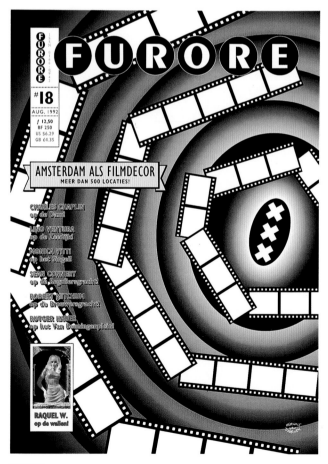

FURORE
Art Director: Piet Schreuders
Designers: Herwolt van Doornen with Piet Schreuders
Publisher: Piet Schreuders

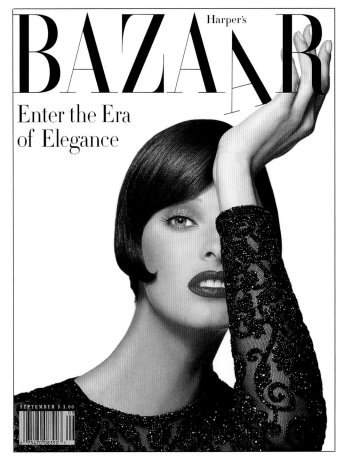

TEMPO
Art Director: Walter Schönauer
Art Consultant: Lo Breier   Photographer: Sheila Rock
Publisher: Jahreszeiten-Verlag

HARPER'S BAZAAR
Creative Director: Fabien Baron, Baron and Baron
Art Director: Joel Berg   Photographer: Patrick Demarchelier
Publisher: Hearst Publications

i-D
Art Director/Designer: Stephen Male
Photographer: Eddie Monsoon
Publisher: Levelprint Ltd.

i-D
Art Director/Designer: Stephen Male
Photographer: Derek Ridgers
Publisher: Levelprint Ltd.

No 92 MAY 1991 £1.80

i-D MAGAZINE
I-DEAS, FASHION, CLUBS, MUSIC, PEOPLE

sister souljah
- new voice of public enemy

de la soul
rap's next step

goa
on the hippy house trail

fashion visionaries
from the london catwalk

how to predict the future

do women have the
right to kill men?

open
your eyes

USA $5.50

9 770262 357006   05

FRANCS 33 LIRE 6.5000 DM 12.50 PESETAS 665 D KR 49

i-D
Art Director/Designer: Stephen Male
Photographer: Renee Valari Cox
Publisher: Levelprint Ltd.

Doubleday Magazine for Book Lovers

D

Volume II, Issue 1
February-May 1993

The Authentic American West
with a Magical, Mythical Spin

Arnold Schwarzenegger:
The *D* Interview

Ruth Prawer Jhabvala's Haunting
Tale of Two Young Women

Morton Hunt on the Maverick
Father of American Psychology

The Compassionate New
Novel from the Author of
Somewhere off the Coast of Maine

Isaac Asimov: A Tribute

A Tragi-comic Love Triangle
from the Author of *White Palace*

The Doubleday Magazine for Book Lovers

D

Volume I, Issue 1
February - May 1992

The Knockout New Thriller
from David Lindsey

Flash, Trash, and Cash:
Nick Tosches on Dean Martin

Jonathan Carroll's New Novel of
Love, Death, and Architecture

An Interview with America's Hottest
New Writer, John Grisham

Sun Dial Street, the Brilliant New Novel
from the Author of *Dying Young*

William Henry III Explores the
Larger-than-Life Life of Jackie Gleason

The Long-awaited New Novel from
the Author of *The River Why*

PREMIERE ISSUE

D
Art Director: Ellen Elchlepp
Illustrator: José Ortega
Publisher: Doubleday

D
Art Director: Ellen Elchlepp
Photographer: Michael McRae
Publisher: Doubleday

WIGWAG
Art Director: Paul Davis
Illustrator: Maira Kalman
Publisher: The Wigwag Magazine Company Inc.

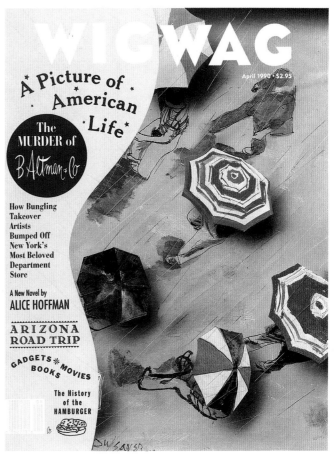

WIGWAG
Art Director: Paul Davis
Illustrator: Robert Weaver
Publisher: The Wigwag Magazine Company Inc.

WIGWAG
Art Director: Paul Davis
Illustrator: Philippe Weisbecker
Publisher: The Wigwag Magazine Company Inc.

WIGWAG
Art Director: Paul Davis
Illustrator: Alexa Grace
Publisher: The Wigwag Magazine Company Inc.

ESQUIRE
Art Director: Rhonda Rubinstein
Illustrator: Barbara Kruger   Photographer: Dave Pokress/Newsday
Publisher: Hearst Magazines

ESQUIRE
Art Director: Rhonda Rubinstein
Photographer: Chris Callis
Publisher: Hearst Magazines

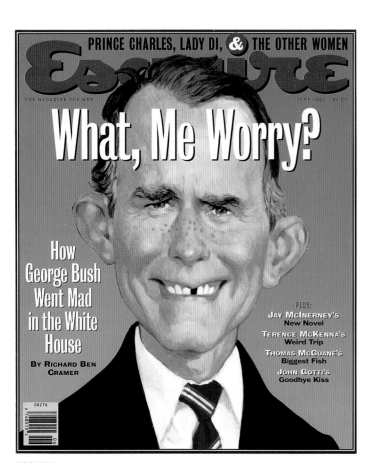

ESQUIRE
Art Director: Rhonda Rubinstein
Illustrator: Richard Williams
Publisher: Hearst Magazines

ESQUIRE
Art Director/Designer: Rhonda Rubinstein
Publisher: Hearst Magazines

ENTERTAINMENT WEEKLY
Design Director: Michael Grossman
Art Director: Mark Michaelson   Photographer: Matthew Rolston
Publisher: Time Inc. Magazine Company

ENTERTAINMENT WEEKLY
Design Director: Michael Grossman
Art Director: Mark Michaelson   Photographer: Mark Hanauer
Publisher: Time Inc. Magazine Company

GRAPHIS
Creative Director: B. Martin Pedersen
Illustrator: Paul Davis
Publisher: Graphis US Inc.

NOVUM GEBRAUCHSGRAPHIK
Designer/Illustrator: Robert Appleton
Publisher: Novum

DIRECTION
Art Director: Mark Porter
Illustrator: Steven Guarnaccia
Publisher: Designers & Art Directors Association

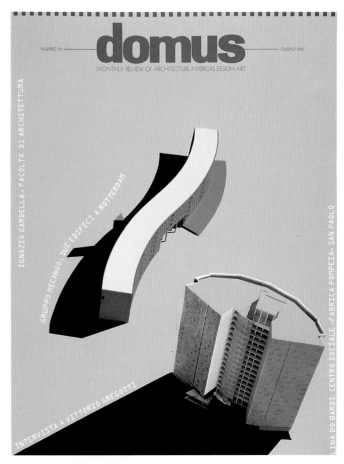

DOMUS
Art Director/Designer: Italo Lupi
Publisher: Editoriale Domus SPA Milano

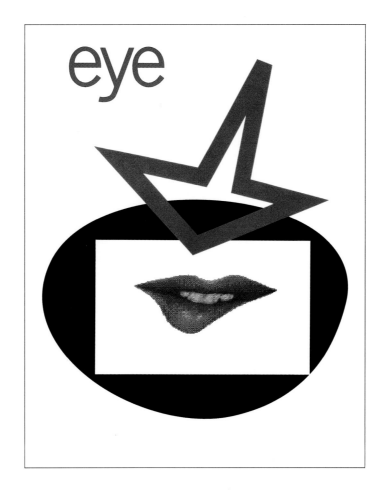

EYE
Art Director: Stephen Coates
Designers: Rick Valicenti and Tony Klassen
Publisher: Wordsearch Ltd.

EYE
Art Director: Stephen Coates
Photographer: Geof Kern
Publisher: Wordsearch Ltd.

U&lc
Art Director: Pentagram
Designer: Woody Pirtle
Publisher: International Typeface Corporation (ITC)

U&lc
Art Director: Pentagram
Designers: Harold Burch and Woody Pirtle
Publisher: International Typeface Corporation (ITC)

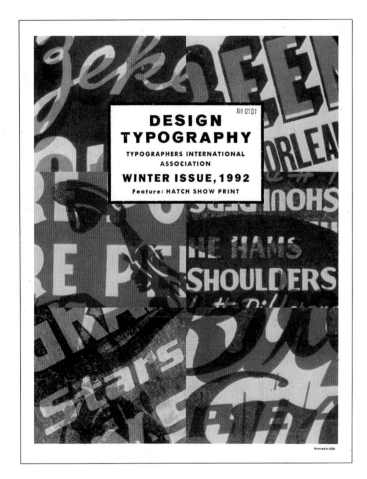

DESIGN TYPOGRAPHY
Art Director: Charles S. Anderson, CS Anderson Design Company
Designers: Charles S. Anderson, Todd Hauswirth and Daniel Olson
Publisher: Typographers International Association (TIA)

FONT & FUNCTION
Art Directors: Gail Blumberg and Susan Verba
Illustrator: Philippe Weisbecker
Publisher: Adobe Systems Inc.

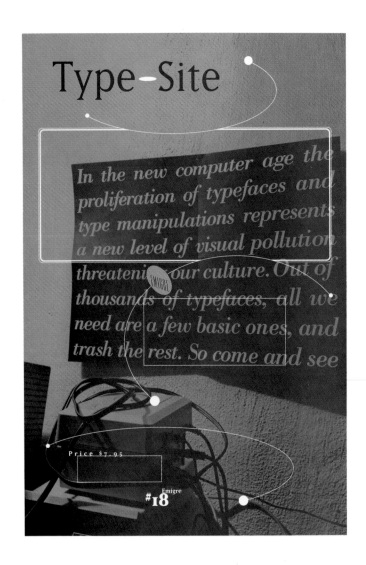

Type-Site

In the new computer age the proliferation of typefaces and type manipulations represents a new level of visual pollution threatening our culture. Out of thousands of typefaces, all we need are a few basic ones, and trash the rest. So come and see

Price $7.95

#18 Emigre

EMIGRE

Culp rits

» ISSUE #23, PRICE $7.95 «

BETTER GRAPHIC DESIGN INSIDE!

EMIGRE
Designer/Photographer: Rudy VanderLans
Publisher: Emigre

EMIGRE
Designer: Rudy VanderLans
Publisher: Emigre

EMIGRE №19: Starting From Zero

Price: $7.95

EMIGRE
Designer: Rudy VanderLans
Publisher: Emigre

ABITARE
Art Director/Designer: Italo Lupi
Illustrator: Anthony Russo
Publisher: L'Editrice Abitare Segesta

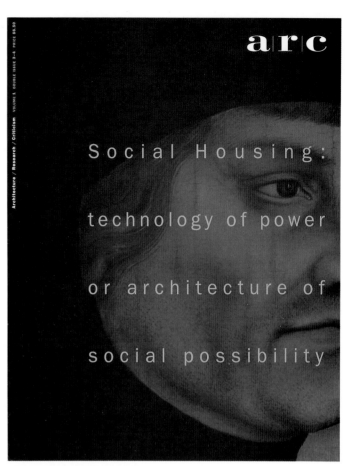

a/r/c
Art Director: Arthur Niemi
Design Firm: Atlanta Art and Design
Publisher: Atlas of the City Publications

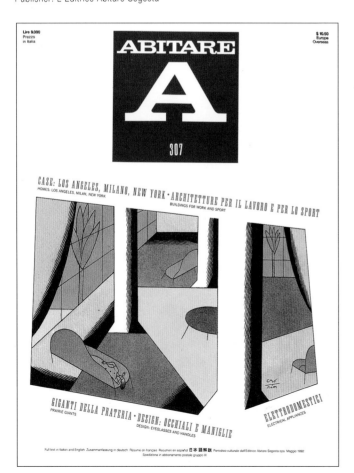

ABITARE
Art Director/Designer: Italo Lupi
Illustrator: Brian Cronin
Publisher: L'Editrice Abitare Segesta

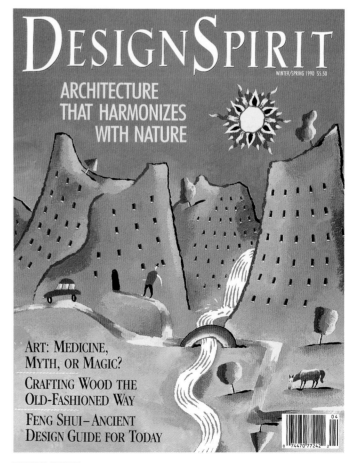

DESIGN SPIRIT
Art Director/Designer: Cynthia Friedman
Illustrator: Jeffrey Fisher
Publisher: Suzanne Koblentz-Goodman

L'ITALIA GRAFICA
Art Director: Bob Noorda
Illustrator: Paolo Guidotti
Publisher: Impricart spa

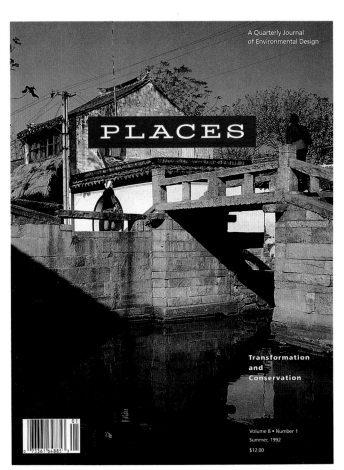

PLACES
Designer: Andre Schutz
Photographer: Joseph C. Wang
Publisher: Design History Foundation

L'ITALIA GRAFICA
Art Director: Bob Noorda
Illustrator: Elisa Lavazza
Publisher: Impricart spa

PLACES
Designer: Andre Schutz
Photographer: Ian MacLeod
Publisher: Design History Foundation

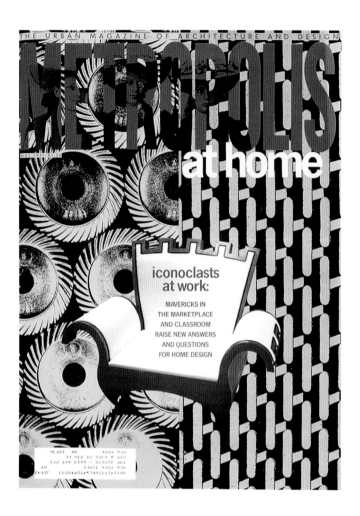

METROPOLIS
Art Directors: Carl Lehmann-Haupt and Nancy Cohen
Publisher: Bellerophon Publications, Inc.

METROPOLIS
Art Directors: Carl Lehmann-Haupt and Nancy Cohen
Photographer: Dan Winters
Publisher: Bellerophon Publications, Inc.

THE URBAN MAGAZINE OF ARCHITECTURE AND DESIGN

METROPOLIS

APRIL 1991 $4.50

View of Washington Heights • A new look at mosaics

Eyeglasses to be seen in • Visions of community

light

ght

revealed

Design/Architecture

METROPOLIS
Art Directors: Carl Lehmann-Haupt and Nancy Cohen
Publisher: Bellerophon Publications, Inc.

RAY GUN
Art Director: David Carson
Illustrator: Larry Carroll   Photographer: Steve Sherman
Publisher: Ray Gun Publishing

RAY GUN
Art Director: David Carson
Photographer: David Simms
Publisher: Ray Gun Publishing

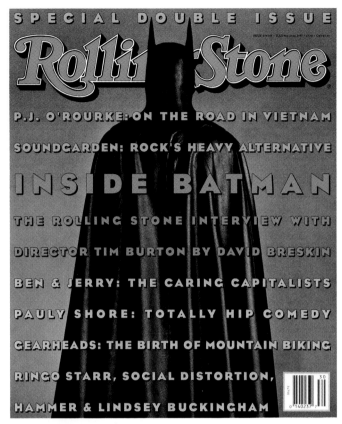

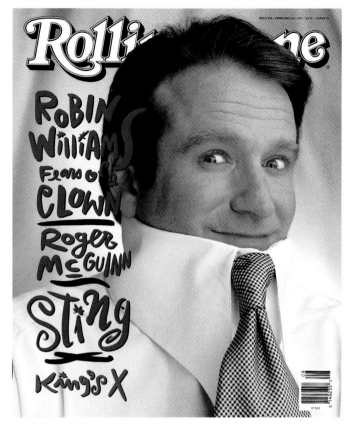

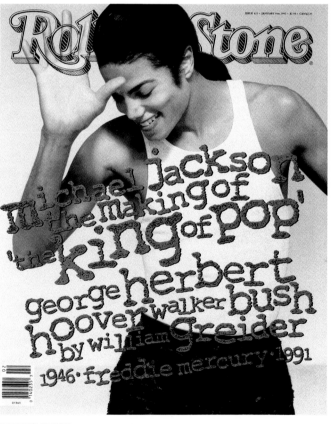

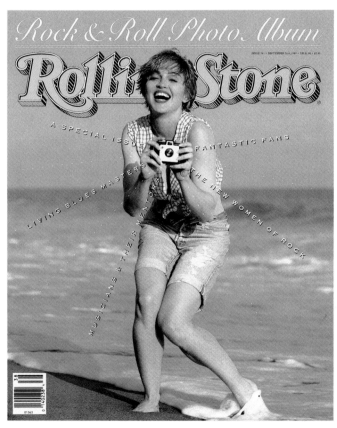

ROLLING STONE
Art Director/Designer: Fred Woodward
Photographer: Herb Ritts
Publisher: Straight Arrow Publishers Inc.

ROLLING STONE
Art Director/Designer: Fred Woodward
Lettering: Laurie Rosenwald   Photographer: Mark Seliger
Publisher: Straight Arrow Publishers Inc.

ROLLING STONE
Art Director/Designer: Fred Woodward
Lettering: Gail Anderson   Photographer: Herb Ritts
Publisher: Straight Arrow Publishers Inc.

ROLLING STONE
Art Director/Designer: Fred Woodward
Photographer: Herb Ritts
Publisher: Straight Arrow Publishers Inc.

Music/Art

153

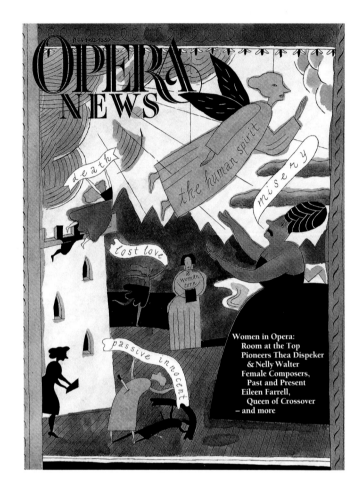

DANCE INK
Art Director: J. Abbott Miller
Photographer: Josef Astor
Publisher: Dance Ink, Inc.

OPERA NEWS
Art Director: Gregory Downer
Illustrator: Jeffrey Fisher
Publisher: Metropolitan Opera Guild

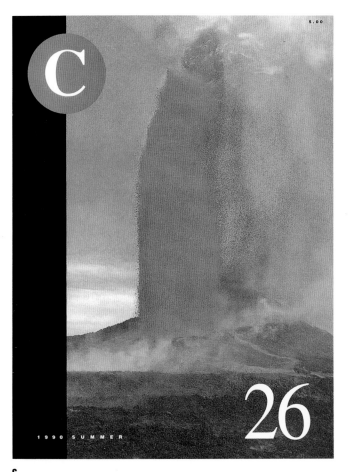

C
Designer: Louis Fishauf
Artist: Roy Arden
Publisher: Arts Publishing & Production, Inc.

BEAUX ARTS
Art Director: Ruedi Baur
Artist: Francis Picabia
Publisher: Publications Nuit et Jour

C
Designer: McCallum Martel
Artist: Mark Gomes   Photographer: Michael Mitchell
Publisher: Arts Publishing & Production, Inc.

PARACHUTE
Designers: Lorti/Mousseau
Artist: Richard Artschwager   Photography: Mary Boone Gallery
Publisher: Parachute Publications

GEO

Uwe George Die Wüste

Vorstoß zu den Grenzen des Lebens

GEO
Art Director: Erwin Ehret
Photographer: Uwe George
Publisher: GEO/Guner & Jahr

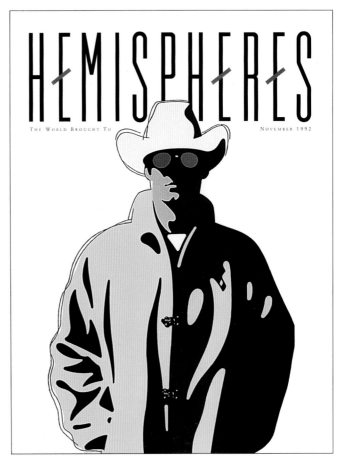

HEMISPHERES
Creative Director/Consultant: Kit Hinricks, Pentagram
Art Director: Jaimey Easler   Illustrator: Ikko Tanaka
Publisher: Pace Communications, Inc.

HEMISPHERES
Art Director: Jaimey Easler
Illustrator: Michael Schwab
Publisher: Pace Communications, Inc.

GEO
Art Director: Erwin Ehret
Designer: Franz Braun   Photographer: Robert Azzi
Publisher: GEO/Guner & Jahr

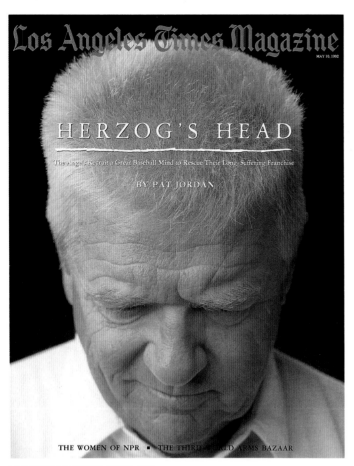

LOS ANGELES TIMES MAGAZINE
Art Director: Nancy Duckworth
Photographer: Mark Seliger
Publisher: Los Angeles Times

LOS ANGELES TIMES MAGAZINE
Art Director: Nancy Duckworth
Illustrator: Gary Baseman
Publisher: Los Angeles Times

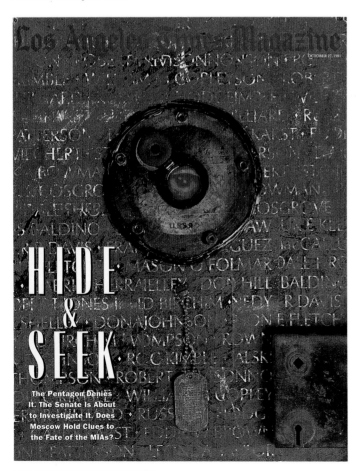

LOS ANGELES TIMES MAGAZINE
Art Director: Nancy Duckworth
Illustrator: Greg Spalenka
Publisher: Los Angeles Times

LOS ANGELES TIMES MAGAZINE
Art Director: Nancy Duckworth
Photographer/Illustrator: William Duke
Publisher: Los Angeles Times

THE WASHINGTON POST MAGAZINE
Art Director: Mark Danzig
Designer: Michael Walch Illustrator: Steven Guarnaccia
Publisher: The Washington Post

THE WASHINGTON POST MAGAZINE
Art Director/Designer: Richard Baker
Photographer: Dixie D. Vereen
Publisher: The Washington Post

THE WASHINGTON POST MAGAZINE
Art Director/Designer: Richard Baker
Illustrator: Marsha Steiger
Publisher: The Washington Post

THE WASHINGTON POST MAGAZINE
Art Director/Designer: Richard Baker
Photographer/Illustrator: Alan Richardson
Publisher: The Washington Post

SUN MAGAZINE
Art Director: Melissa Brown
Illustrator: Anita Kunz
Publisher: The Baltimore Sun

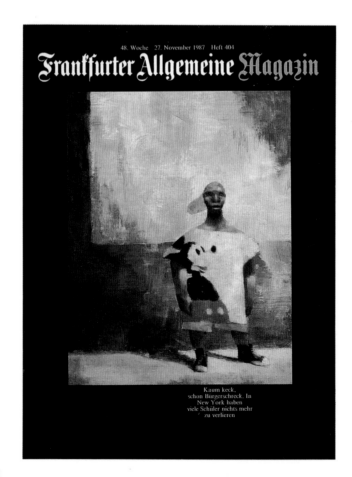

FRANKFURTER ALLGEMEINE MAGAZIN
Art Director: Hans Geog Pospischil
Illustrator: Brad Holland
Publisher: Frankfurter Allgemeine Zeitung

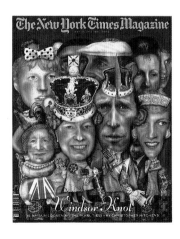

The New York Times Magazine
Art Director: Janet Froelich
Illustrators: *(left)* Wiktor Sadowski, *(middle)* Janet Wooley, *(right)* Charles Burns
Photographer: *(top)* Mary Ellen Mark
Publisher: The New York Times Company

CHARLESTON MAGAZINE
Art Director: Jaimey Easler
Illustrator: Jonathan Green
Publisher: Gulfstream Communications, Inc.

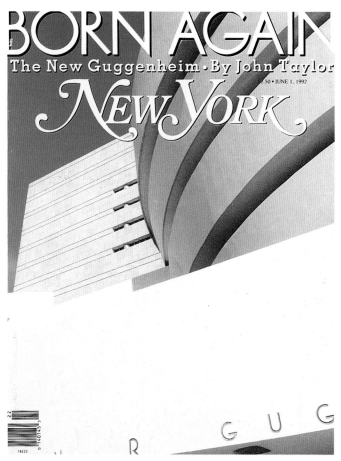

NEW YORK
Design Director: Robert Best
Photographer: Ted Hardin
Publisher: K-III Magazine Corporation

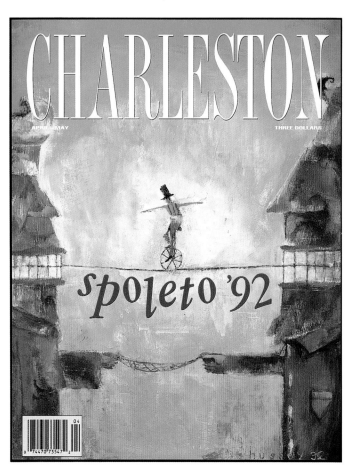

CHARLESTON MAGAZINE
Art Director: Jaimey Easler
Illustrator: Timothy Hussey
Publisher: Gulfstream Communications, Inc.

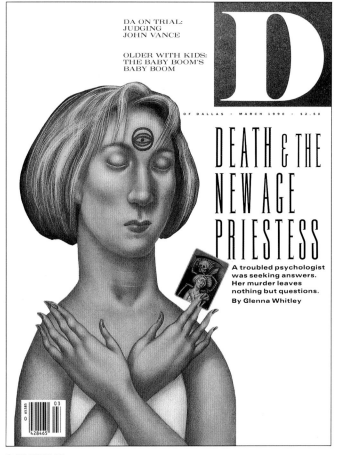

D OF DALLAS
Art Director: Steve Connatfer
Illustrator: Anita Kunz
Publisher: American Express Publishing Corporation

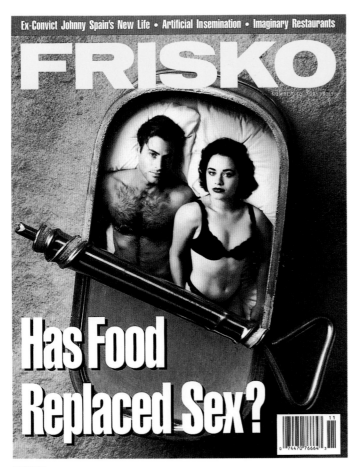

FRISKO
Creative Director: William Katovsky
Art Director: Nancy Terzian   Photographer: Erik Butler
Publisher: Frisko Magazine Inc.

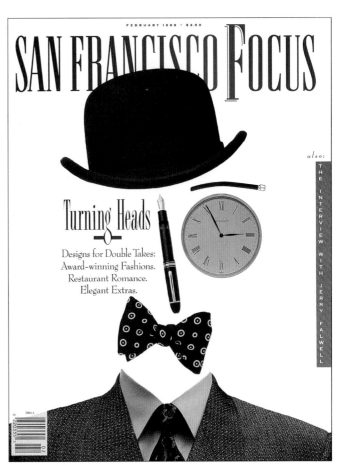

SAN FRANCISCO FOCUS
Art Director/Designer: Matthew Drace
Photographer: David Peterson
Publisher: KQED, Inc.

SAN FRANCISCO FOCUS
Art Director/Designer: Matthew Drace
Illustrator/Typographer: Tim Carroll
Publisher: KQED, Inc.

SAN FRANCISCO FOCUS
Art Director/Designer: Matthew Drace
Illustrator: Michael Schwab
Publisher: KQED, Inc.

TIME INTERNATIONAL
Art Director: Rudolph C. Hoglund
Graphics Director: Nigel Holmes   Illustrator: Mirko Ilic
Publisher: Time Inc.

TIME INTERNATIONAL
Art Director/Illustrator: Mirko Ilic
Publisher: Time Inc.

TIME
Art Director: Mirko Ilic
Designer: Louise Fili   Illustrator: Mark Summers
Publisher: Time Inc.

TIME
Art Director: Mirko Ilic
Photographer: Mark Peterson, JB Pictures
Publisher: Time Inc.

TIME

INTERNATIONAL

**Does it exist — or
do bad things just happen?**

News

AUSTRIA . . . . S 30	FRANCE . . . . F 17.00	IRELAND (incl. tax) . . . IR£1.50	NORWAY . . . . Kr 17.00	SWITZERLAND . . . . . . F 4.00
BELGIUM . . . . F 100	GERMANY . . . . . . DM 4.80	ISRAEL (incl. tax) . . . . NS 5.90	POLAND . . . . . PLZ 18000.00	TURKEY (incl. tax) . . . TL 6000
CZECHOSLOVAKIA . CZC 35.00	GIBRALTAR £1.50	ITALY . . . . Lit 3300	PORTUGAL . . . . Esc 350	UNITED KINGDOM £1.30
CYPRUS . . . . CP 1.30	GREECE . . . . Dr 400	LUXEMBOURG . . . . . . F 100	ROMANIA . . . . . . ROL 50.00	U.S. ARMED FORCES . . . $2.35
DENMARK . . . . Kr 18.00	HUNGARY . . . . HUF 120.00	MALTA 80c	SPAIN . . . . Pta 325	U.S.S.R. . . . . SUR 4.00
FINLAND . . . . MK 18.00	ICELAND (incl. tax) . Kr 160.00	NETHERLANDS . . . . . Fl 5.00	SWEDEN (incl. tax) . Kr 17.00	YUGOSLAVIA . . . . . ND 55.00
				WEEKLY

TIME INTERNATIONAL
Art Director/ Type Designer: Mirko Ilic
Designer: Arthur Hochstein
Publisher: Time Inc.

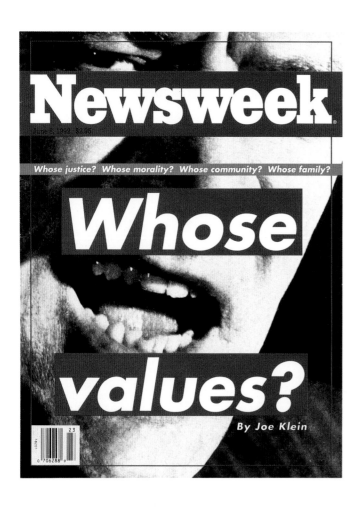

NEWSWEEK
Creative Director: Patricia Bradbury
Art Director: Ron Meyerson   Illustrator: Barbara Kruger
Publisher: Newsweek Inc.

NEWSWEEK
Creative Director: Patricia Bradbury
Art Director: Ron Meyerson   Illustrator: Anita Kunz
Publisher: Newsweek Inc.

THE ATLANTIC
Art Director: Judy Garlan
Illustrator: Kinuko Craft
Publisher: The Atlantic Monthly Co.

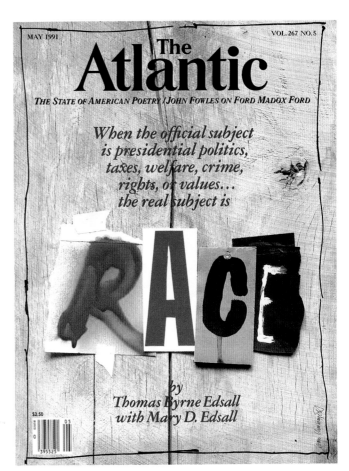

THE ATLANTIC
Art Director: Judy Garlan
Illustrator: Ivan Chermayeff
Publisher: The Atlantic Monthly Co.

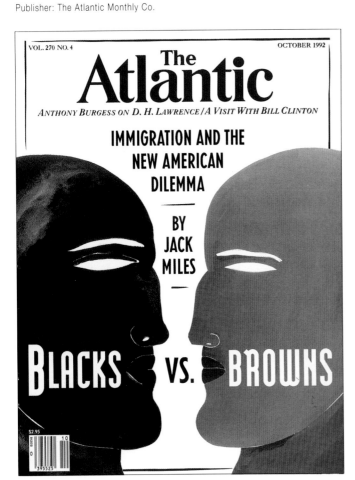

THE ATLANTIC
Art Director: Judy Garlan
Illustrator: Karen Barbour
Publisher: The Atlantic Monthly Co.

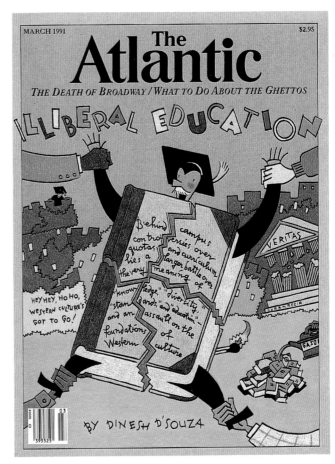

THE ATLANTIC
Art Director: Judy Garlan
Illustrator: Steven Guarnaccia
Publisher: The Atlantic Monthly Co.

MOTHER JONES
Art Director: Kerry Tremain
Illustrator: Melissa Grimes
Publisher: Foundation for National Progress

MOTHER JONES
Art Director: Kerry Tremain
Illustrator: Anita Kunz
Publisher: Foundation for National Progress

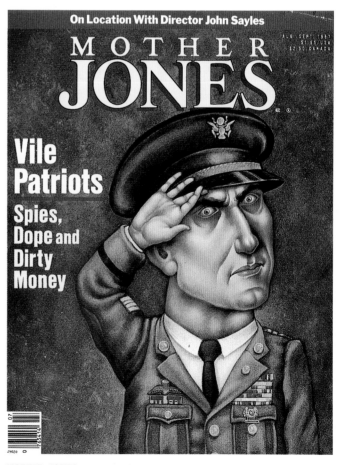

MOTHER JONES
Art Director: Louise Kollenbaum
Illustrator: Anita Kunz
Publisher: Foundation for National Progress

FEBRUARY 27, 1989 · $2.25

Gorbachev's Secret Weapon: Reaganomics

SDI GROUPIES · A HISTORY OF CHILD DESERTION · KAUFFMANN ON HOLLYWOOD'S GOLDEN AGE

WHY I'LL
MISS
LYNDON
LAROUCHE
—ALEX HEARD

THE NEW REPUBLIC

Bird's True Colors

*Behind the myths
of Charlie Parker
by Stanley Crouch*

09

787445

News

THE NEW REPUBLIC
Art Director: Mark Stevens
Illustrator: Paul Davis
Publisher: The New Republic Inc.

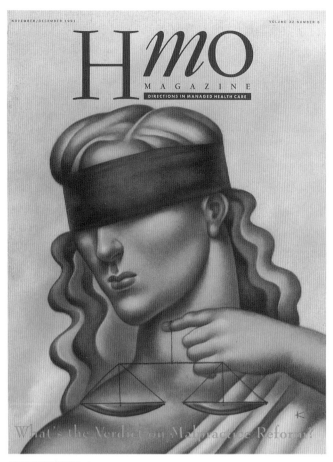

HMO MAGAZINE

Art Director/Designer: Nancy Steiny
Illustrator: Anita Kunz
Publisher: Group Health Association of America

The Bigger Picture

PACIFIC

Art Director/Designer: Michael Mabry Design
Illustrator: Steven Guarnaccia
Publisher: Pacific Telesis Group

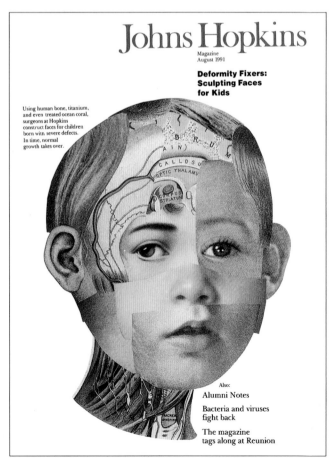

Johns Hopkins
Magazine
August 1991

**Deformity Fixers:
Sculpting Faces
for Kids**

Using human bone, titanium,
and even treated ocean coral,
surgeons at Hopkins
construct faces for children
born with severe defects.
In time, normal
growth takes over.

Also:
Alumni Notes

Bacteria and viruses
fight back

The magazine
tags along at Reunion

JOHNS HOPKINS MAGAZINE

Art Director: Royce Faddis
Designer: Claude Skelton   Illustrator: Melissa Grimes
Publisher: The Johns Hopkins University

*New
Information
Pathways*

PACIFIC

Art Director/Designer: Michael Mabry Design
Illustrator: Steven Guarnaccia
Publisher: Pacific Telesis Group

FOUR SEASONS
Art Director: Mark Koudys, Atlanta Art and Design
Photographer: Eden Robbins
Publisher: Four Seasons, Hotels and Resorts

FOUR SEASONS
Art Director: Mark Koudys, Atlanta Art and Design
Photographers: John Lloyd and Nancy Saxberg
Publisher: Four Seasons, Hotels and Resorts

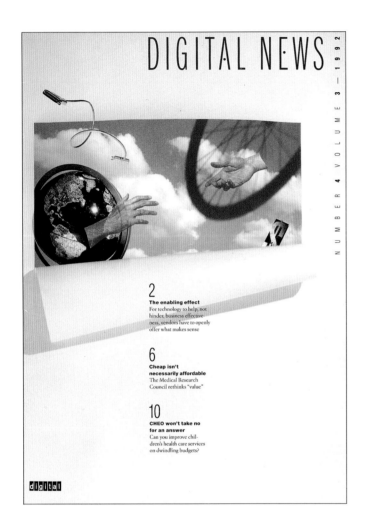

DIGITAL NEWS
Art Director: Mark Koudys, Atlanta Art and Design
Photographer: Ron Baxter Smith
Publisher: Digital Equipment of Canada Ltd.

DIGITAL NEWS
Art Director: Mark Koudys, Atlanta Art and Design
Illustrator: Gene Greif
Publisher: Digital Equipment of Canada Ltd.

ALDUS
Art Director: J. Scott Campbell
Designer: Becky Sundling
Publisher: Aldus Corporation

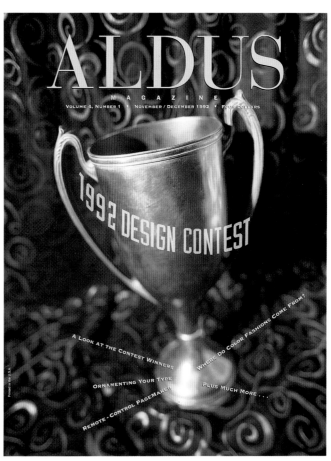

ALDUS
Art Director/Designer: Kristin Easterbrook
Photographer: Abrams/Lacagnina
Publisher: Aldus Corporation

ALDUS
Art Director/Designer: Kristin Easterbrook
Illustrator: Scott Matthews
Publisher: Aldus Corporation

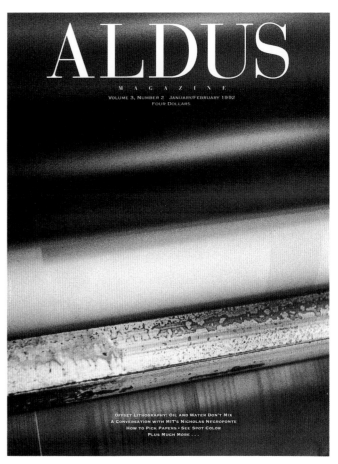

ALDUS
Art Director: J. Scott Campbell
Photographer: Abrams/Lacaguina
Publisher: Aldus Corporation

blu r
Art Director: Scott Clum
Illustrators: Gavin Wilson and Jon Jensen
Photographer: Trevor Graves   Publisher: Ride

blu r
Art Director: Scott Clum
Illustrators: Gavin Wilson and Jon Jensen
Photographer: Trevor Graves   Publisher: Ride

Jim Morrison: Spoil the Rod and Despair

MONDO

Issue No. 4 $5.95   Canada $6.95

Brian Eno

D'Cückoo

Burroughs &
Leary Together

MONDO 2000
Designer: Bart Nagel
Photographer: Stephanie Rausser
Publisher: Funcity Megamedia

MONDO 2000
Designer: Bart Nagel
Illustrator: Eric White
Publisher: Funcity Megamedia

RUBBER BLANKET
Art Director: David Mazzucchelli
Designers: David Mazzucchelli and Richmond Lewis
Publisher: Rubber Blanket Press

RUBBER BLANKET
Art Director: David Mazzucchelli
Designers: David Mazzucchelli and Richmond Lewis
Publisher: Rubber Blanket Press

THE NOSE
Art Director/Designer: Bart Nagel
Photography: White House Photo
Publisher: Acme Publishing Inc.

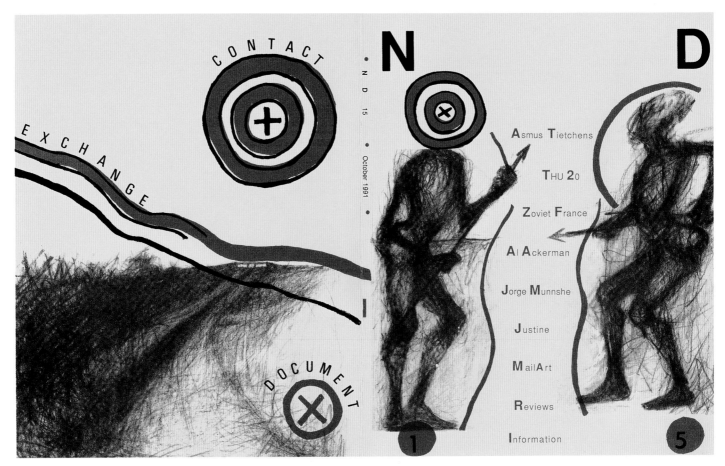

N D
Art Director: Dan Plunkett
Illustrator: Amanda Waggoner
Publisher: Daniel Plunkett, N D

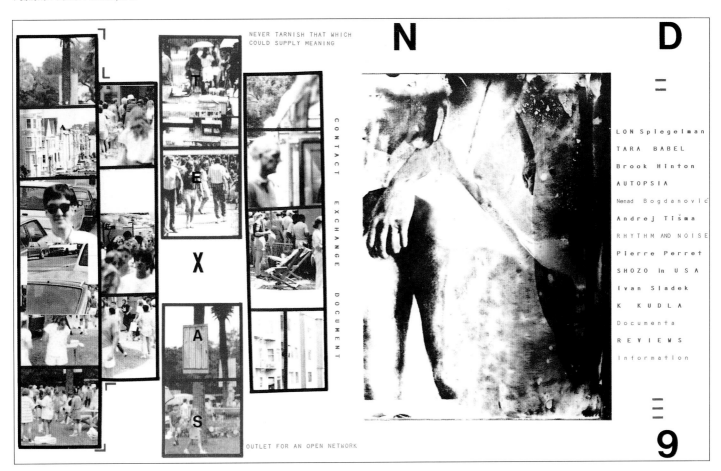

N D
Art Director: Dan Plunkett
Photographer: Ivan Sladek
Publisher: Daniel Plunkett, N D

NOZONE
Art Director: Knickerbocker
Illustrator: Gary Baseman
Publisher: Nozone

NOZONE
Art Director: Knickerbocker
Illustrator: Seymour Chwast
Publisher: Nozone

2029 magazin

architektur

& design

2029 MAGAZIN
Designers: Christof Rabanus and Ray Nher
Illustrator: Yvonne Bargstadt
Publisher: 2029 Magazin Verlag

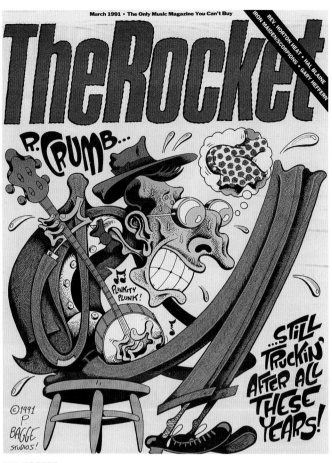

THE ROCKET
Art Director/Designer: Art Chantry
Illustrator: Peter Bagge
Publisher: Murder, Inc.

THE ROCKET
Art Director/Designer: Art Chantry
Illustrator: Stan Shaw
Publisher: Murder, Inc.

THE ROCKET
Art Director/Designer: Art Chantry
Illustrator: Nathan Gluck
Publisher: Murder, Inc.

CREDITS

APPENDIX

Abitare
Editrice
Abitare Segesta s.p.a.
corso Montforte
20122 Milano
Italia

Harry N. Abrams Inc.
100 Fifth Avenue
New York, NY 10011

Aldus Magazine
Aldus Corporation
411 First Avenue South
Seattle, WA 98104-2871
Kristin Easterbrook/Art Director

Charles Anderson
30 North First Street
Minneapolis, MN 55401

Appleton Design
488 Fern Street
West Hartford, CT 06107

The Atlantic
745 Boylston Street
Boston, MA 02116
Judy Garlan/Art Director

Atlantic Monthly Press
19 Union Square West
New York, NY 10003

Harper's Bazaar
1700 Broadway
New York, NY 10019
Fabien Baron/Creative Director

Black Sparrow Press
24 Tenth Street
Santa Rosa, CA 95401

BlackDog
239 Main Street
San Rafael, CA 94901

blu r
P.O. Box 484
Salem, OR 97308-484
Scott Clum/Art Director

Peter Bradford
11 East 22nd Street
New York, NY 10010

c magazine of contemporary art
P.O. Box 5, Station B
Toronto, Ontario
Canada M5T 2T2
Joyce Mason & Carol Peaker/Art Directors

Jonathan Cape Limited
20 Vauxhall Bridge Road
London, SW1V 2SA
England

Peter Dyer/Art Director
Art Chantry Design
P.O. Box 4069
Seattle, WA 98104

Chronicle Books
275 Fifth Street
San Francisco, CA 94103
Michael Carabetta/Art Director

Marc Cohen
Eight Mosswood Terrace
Maplewood, NJ 07040

Clarkson Potter
201 East 50th Street
New York, NY 10022
Howard Klein/Art Director

Dance Ink
145 Central Park West
New York, NY 10023
Patsy Tarr/Publisher

Paul Davis Studio
14 East Fourth Street
New York, NY 10003

Doubleday
666 Fifth Avenue
New York, NY 10103

Drenttel Doyle Partners
1123 Broadway, Suite 600
New York, NY 10010

Emigre
4475 D Street
Sacramento, CA 95819
Rudy VanderLans/Publisher

Entertainment Weekly
1675 Broadway
New York, NY 10019
Michael Grossman/Art Director

Esquire
1790 Broadway
New York, NY 10019

Farrar Straus Giroux
19 Union Square West
New York, NY 10003
Dorris Janowitz/Art Director

Louise Fili Ltd.
22 West 19th Street
New York, NY 10011

Fjord Press
P.O. Box 16349
Seattle, WA 98116

Font & Function
1585 Charleston Road
P.O. Box 7900
Mountain View, CA 94039-7900

Frisko
1736 Stockton Street
San Francisco, CA 94133
Nancy Terzian/Art Director

Geo
Gruner + Jahr AG & Co.
Postfach 11 00 11
2000 Hamburg 36
Germany

Erwin Ehret/Art Director
Carin Goldberg
26 West 20th Street
New York, NY 10011

Graphis
141 Lexington Avenue
New York, NY 10016

Graphiti
Progettazioni
visive s.n.c.
Via Faetina 69
50133 Firenze
Italia

Grove Weidenfeld
841 Broadway
New York, NY 10003-4793
Krystyna Skalski/Art Director

Melissa Grimes
901 Cumberland
Austin, TX 78704

Steven Guarnaccia
430 West 14th Street
New York, NY 10014

Hard Werken Design BV
P.O. Box 25058
3001 HB Rotterdam
The Netherlands

Hemispheres
1301 Carolina Street
Greensboro, NC 27401
Jaimey Easler/Art Director

i-D Magazine
Fifth floor, seven dials warehouse
44 Earlham Street
London WC2H 9LA
England
Stephen Male/Art Director

Interview
575 Broadway
New York, NY 10012
Richard Pandiscio/Art Director

L'Italia Grafica
Piazza della Concihazione 1
20123 Milano
Italia

Alfred A. Knopf Publishers
201 East 50th Street
New York, NY 10022
Carol Carson/Art Director

Anita Kunz
230 Ontario Street
Toronto
Ontario M5A 2V5
Canada

Molly Leach
43 West 16th Street, No. 1E
New York, NY 10011

Lire
38 Avenue Hoche
75008 Paris
France

Los Angeles Times Magazine
Times Mirror Square
Los Angeles, CA 90053
Nancy Duckworth/Art Director

Dr. Architetto Italo Lupi
39 Via Vigevano
20144 Milano
Italia

Michael Mabry Design
212 Sutter Street
San Francisco, CA 94108

Macmillan Publishing Company
866 Third Avenue
New York, NY 10022
Susan Newman/Associate Art Director

Fred Marcellino
432 Park Avenue South
New York, NY 10016

Rita Marshall
Route 44
Lakeville, CT 06039

James McMullan
222 Park Avenue South, Apt. 10B
New York, NY 10003

Metropolis
177 East 87th Street
New York, NY 10128
Carl Lehmann-Haupt/Art Director

Mondo 2000
P.O. Box 10171
Berkeley, CA 94709-5171
Bart Nagel/Art Director

Mother Jones
1663 Mission Street
San Francisco, CA 94103-2499

N D
P.O. Box 4144
Austin, TX 78765
Daniel Plunkett/Editor

New York
755 Second Avenue
New York, NY 10017

New York Times Magazine
229 West 43rd Street
New York, NY 10036

The Nose
1095 Market Street
San Francisco, CA 94103
Bart Nagel/Art Director

Pantheon Books
201 East 50th Street
New York, NY 10022

Parachute
4060, Boulevard St. Laurent
Bureau 501, Montreal
Quebec, H2W 1Y9
Canada
Colette Tougas/Managing Editor

Penguin USA
375 Hudson Street
New York, NY 10014
Michael Ian Kaye/Art Director

Pentagram
11 Needham Road
London W11 2RP
England
John McConnell/Partner

Pentagram
212 Fifth Avenue
New York, NY 10010

Places
The Design History Foundation
110 Higgins Hall
Pratt Institute School of Architecture
200 Willoughby Avenue
Brooklyn, NY 11205

Pocket Books
1230 Avenue of the Americas
New York, NY 10020

Poseidon Press
1230 Avenue of the Americas
New York, NY 10020

Premiere
23-25, rue de Berri
75388 Paris Cedex 08
France
Xavier Boure/Art Director

Random House Inc.
201 East 50th Street
New York, NY 10022

Rolling Stone
745 Fifth Avenue
New York, NY 10022
Fred Woodward/Art Director

Rubber Blanket
Rubber Blanket Press
P.O. Box 3067
Uptown Station
Hoboken, NJ 07030

Anthony Russell Associates
584 Broadway, Suite 701
New York, NY 10012

San Francisco Focus
2601 Mariposa
San Francisco, CA 94110-1400
Mark Ulriksen/Art Director

St. Martin's Press
175 Fifth Avenue
New York, NY 10010

Schocken Books
201 East 50th Street
New York, NY 10022

Piet Schreuders
Hartenstraat 26/2
1016 CC Amsterdam
The Netherlands

Michael Schwab
80 Liberty Ship Way No. 7
Sausalito, CA 94965

Se Studio Editoriale SRL
Via Manin 13
20121 Milano
Italia

Senate Design Ltd
One Princeton Court
55 Felsham Road
London SW15 1AZ
England

Keith Sheridan Associates Inc.
236 West 27th Street
New York, NY 10001

Simon & Schuster
1230 Avenue of the Americas
New York, NY 10020

Stewart Tabori & Chang
575 Broadway
New York, NY 10012

Travel & Leisure
1120 Avenue of the Americas
New York, NY 10036
Lloyd Ziff/Art Director

Stephanie Tevonian
417 Canal Street
New York, NY 10013

Jon Valk
245 East 24th Street
New York, NY 10010

Vintage Books
201 East 50th Street
New York, NY 10022
Susan Mitchell/Art Director

WBMG Inc.
207 East 32nd Street
New York, NY 10016

Warner Books
1271 Avenue of the Americas
New York, NY 10020
Jackie Merri Meyer/Art Director

Washington Post Magazine
1150 15th Street NW
Washington DC 20071
Richard Baker/Art Director

Philippe Weisbecker
136 Waverly Place
New York, NY 10014

William Morrow & Co. Inc.
1350 Avenue of the Americas
New York, NY 10019
Bob Aulicino/Art Director

Lloyd Ziff
55 Van Dam Street
New York, NY 10013

INDEX

ARTISTS

PHOTOGRAPHERS

THE MAGAZINE

ILLUSTRATORS

PHOTOGRAPHERS

ACKNOWLEDGMENTS

Sincere gratitude goes to Susan Kapsis our editor at PBC for shepherding this project with wisdom, good humor, and of course, patience. Thanks to Kevin Clark, editorial director new title development, and Penny Sibal, managing director, for inviting us to do this book. Thanks to Joanne Caggiano, Karen Chandler, Debra Harding, Richard Liu, and Garrett Schuh for all their support. And to Stephanie Tevonian for her excellent art direction and design.